SELLING THE WAY YOUR CUSTOMER BUYS

"Learning how to have your prospects ask for the Order"

Revised 2013

By: Marvin C Sadovsky, PhD

Table of Contents

Introduction

Imagine the number of sales you could close if you developed deep rapport with each of your clients. What if you could easily understand what drives them, discover what they like to hear, determine the exact sales strategy that will get you the best results? Well, it is not just a dream any more. You actually can tap into a client's unconscious thought patterns. Selling The Way Your Customer Buys shows you how.

By following this revolutionary new selling system, you will learn to ask the right questions, and then decipher the answers to get an accurate reading on each person's motivations, desires, and buying behavior. You will learn how to close exactly the way a client or customer makes a decision to buy. Here is what a client of mine, Rex Dixon, senior vice president, global sales, Harding International, had to say about this book. "The book underscores what skilled sales and marketing executives realize people today do not like to be sold to. The selling salesperson is rapidly and thankfully becoming extinct. Today, knowing your customer is paramount to continued success. Selling The Way Your Customer Buys will enable you to reach new and incredibly profitable levels. Dr. Sadovsky, author and managing director of Leadership Strategy, LLC presents a revised edition of the original book published under a similar title by AMACOM Publishing in 1996. The original book was edited and co-authored with Jon Caswell.

Chapter 1
Gaining Deep Rapport

If you have ever lost a sale knowing that somehow rapport was broken and not knowing the reason, this book is a way to never experience that again. If you follow the simple rules of a natural persuasion, selling will be a simple service and value added experience. If you had never lost a sale, you might be relaxing somewhere where enjoying the fruits of your new natural closing skills. However, you are probably reading this book because you ring up more No Sales than Sales. You can try to convince yourself that selling is a numbers game, but we all know there is more to it.

Making a sale can be very personal because we make a connection when we succeed. You can sense when something happens between you and the client. Why aren't all sales calls that way? We have all lost sales, and when we did, which one of us did not want to climb inside the customer's head to understand how they perceived the transaction? What better way than to learn what we did wrong, or right. Did they dislike your visual presentation? Would they have thrived on simple phone contact, or did they expect you to come in, ask about the golf game or the family?

What convinced them to go with your competitor? What motivated them suddenly to decide after months of seeming to do nothing? "Selling The Way Your Customer Buys" opens the doorway into your client's mind. With a few simple questions that you can easily weave into any conversation, you'll learn to uncover your customer' unconscious mental blueprints, not the deep secrets of childhood, mind you, but the background patterns that keep them oriented and functioning in our complicated world. You will find an unconscious template with which they operate the computer we call the human brain. At one level, the person across the desk is as predictable as a laptop.

Just as every computer has a disk operating system, or DOS, your customer has an operating system that functions in the background. This unconscious background program we call BOS for Behavioral Operating System. This Behavioral Operating System is composed of many elements and operates in every aspect of our lives. Each component of the BOS is made up of patterns. These patterns drive our behavior. When you feel synchronized with someone, what we call "deep rapport" in this book, you have matched one or more of these unconscious patterns. The BOS patterns are strategies and concepts that drive our conscious feelings and actions.

When we access these unconscious cues, people naturally feel comfortable with us and trust who we are and what we represent. In essence, rapport is having your behavior perfectly understood, and returned to you with a similar response. You do not have to agree, all you have to do is feedback the other person's truth. Rapport satisfies like no other human experience. Unfortunately, the likelihood of your matching with someone else in more than one category is not very good. Researchers have identified more than 50 behavior categories, BOS components, and each category contains at least two patterns, often more. So the possible combinations quickly run into the millions. The odds of naturally matching every component of your customer's Behavioral Operating System are astronomical.

Please keep this in mind as you consider these odds. You're betting your paycheck. Sometimes only a single mismatch in one of these categories turns a sale sour. No wonder the average sales close is only one out of eight. The problem is that most people haven't a clue about accessing these unconscious cues. If you asked a person outright what their cues were, they could not answer you even if they understood the question. However, if you ask the right questions, questions designed to expose the patterns and know what to listen for; they will present BOS strategies and concepts with surprising clarity. This book contains BOS questions and the key to deciphering the information they elicit. We have simplified the identification of BOS patterns by clustering eight BOS components that relate to buying behavior.

Knowing your client's BOS program improves your odds because you can quickly get into the zone of deep rapport by matching their unconscious strategies. You run no risk. You can even identify every one of the BOS eight buying patterns over the phone. We have observed the power of this knowledge countless times in real time, real-world sales scenarios. Here is an example. Michael, one of our clients, sells financial products. He had worked with a couple for three months trying to sell them a retirement program, a million dollar transaction. The couple and Michael had a relationship that went back several years, and he felt they trusted him, especially since they had made the initial contact. However, meeting after meeting, he could not get them to commit. Finally, he called us for advice.

After a brief conversation, we suggested he change the structure of his presentation. Up to that point, he had made all the variables of the program equal and left the decision completely up to them. Not a bad strategy, but one that violated one of the couple's basic BOS components and kept them from trusting Michael. In the language of the BOS program, they sorted externally.

6

Without a concrete suggestion from the salesperson that they unconsciously viewed as the expert, they were lost. In their buying strategy program, a salesperson without a suggestion equaled a person who lacked commitment to the product. Instinctively, they did not want choices; they wanted guidance. That is why they had called Michael, a friend, instead of going through the Yellow Pages. However, just as instinctively, Michael, whose pattern was internal, thought they would want to decide for themselves as he would have, rather than have him insert his opinion on such an important deal.

What he viewed as an intrusion, they viewed as a necessary component of the transaction. When Michael changed his presentation to indicate clearly, which alternatives were best for the couple, they bought immediately. Think of your client's brain as a computer that you're trying to access. You are sitting at the keyboard and you start typing on the keys. Nothing happens, because you don't know what program he's running, so you don't know which keys do what. To remedy that, you pull out the template from your own computer, and put it on his keyboard and begin typing happily away. Again, nothing happens. There is no sale because your customer's brain is running a different program, HIS. Your keyboard template does not match his pattern so you are pushing all the wrong buttons. Only by sheer luck or profound determination would you ever be able to decipher the commands necessary to operate his computer.

The BOS program allows you to tap into the buying program of every one of your customers. No longer will they seem mysterious. When you know their BOS programs, you will be able to give them information in the individual and unique ways in which they most readily accept it. You will create deep rapport with them because you will press the right keys for the outcome you want. Your closure rate will definitely increase. You will have the time of your life with sales from customers who think you are one of the finest people they have ever met. And, you are, because you know How To Sell The Way Your Customer Buys.

Here is an important note. The BOS program is context-specific. Each of the following chapters revolved around a single question. The emphasized portion represents the formula of the question, and should remain the same. The context can be changed to make it appropriate for your situation. For example, notice the question from **Chapter 2**. <u>For you, what's important about</u> [selling the product, the service, working, relationships, eating lunch, going to church]? Each one of these particular endings, the context of the question will elicit different responses because we all may have different values in the BOS.

The information you derive from the question only applies within the context in which the question was asked. You control that context according to how you frame the question. BOS information cannot be generalized between contexts. Thus, when adapting these questions for your repertoire of sales tools, change the contextual part of the question to fit your circumstances.

Chapter 2
Words that Motivate Your Customer

If you have ever visited a foreign country, you can easily recall the affinity you felt for people who could speak your language. Even in our country, the specialized language we share often defines the groups we belong to: in our houses of worship, jobs, sports, and home. All of us use words to which we have attached personal and unique meanings. These words or phrases represent our values in a given context. These are the result of our individual experiences. The words themselves actually connect the person to the emotional experience, which in turn stimulates chemicals to flow in the brain, and these results in motivation.

Without motivation, nothing happens, no rapport, no sale, no money. Therefore, you can see how critical words can be, and that's why we call this category of the Behavioral Operating System, motivating language. These words reflect what we feel is important. They are as individual as fingerprints. When these specific words, not their synonyms, are used, we respond with increased attention because we connect significance to them. For a general example, let's use the context of baseball which has a very specialized language. Visualize a runner stealing second. He is speeding over the base path as fast as he can. The catcher springs from behind the plate. The pitcher jumps to one side as the ball sails straight over the mount. The second baseman moves into position, snags the throw, and puts the tag on runner as he slides into the bag. Safe or out? Everybody's attention locks on the umpire who cocks his thumb over his should and yells, "He's out." With one word, "out," the umpire make the offense unhappy and the defense ecstatic. Another way to say that is he has destroyed rapport with the base

9

runner and his team. By calling the runner out, he has met the defense team's criteria for happiness, and by doing so, has created rapport with them. Using the right words and phrases goes along way in creating rapport, the essential step in sales synergy.

Unfortunately, the BOS words and phrases are not as clear-cut in most sales situations as "safe" or "out." Everywhere we interact with people, we create a special vocabulary that both generates and defines the relationships. Our special words keep strangers outside the gates, and identify the BOS we allow to pass. When you know the motivating language of another person, you have a key to that gate. In a selling situation, these power words represent your customer's criteria for purchase. When you meet the BOS criteria, they will almost certainly buy. These criteria words and phrases reflect our core belief systems about the particular context. This is why the exact words are so powerful. They touch us at a deep level. Criteria words are power words.

When we hear them, we naturally feel interested and predisposed to listening. If you want someone to feel drawn to what you have to offer, match their criteria words to your ideas and watch how quickly they take to heart what you have to say. Few people realize the power of this kind of matched speech. Although, very subtle, its impact is almost irresistible. When you use another person's words and phrases, you create rapport with them, and that is the essential step in sales synergy.

The question for motivating language. Please answer this question on a sheet of paper or speak the answer into a recorder. For you, what is really important about [context....]? When you ask this question of a client, be sure to use the formula and insert the appropriate context, buying a car, a stereo, going to lunch, getting married,

10

having a job, selling. It is important to qualify the question with "for you." Otherwise, you may get a general answer that will not give you the person's power words. You fill in the context.

How to interpret what you hear? The specific words contained in the answer are important. You must remember words exactly and use them in the same manner they were used. Synonyms or interpretations will not have the desired affect. When your client answers the question, pay attention to the emphasized words your prospect uses. These are power words. Feel free to ask the question for several contexts, a specific service or product, lunch, movies, any area where you would like to have influence. As we all know, having influence is a necessary precondition to making a sale, for if you cannot influence your client, how can your input sway their decision in your favor?

If you are on the phone when you ask this question, jot down the exact answer. The criteria words will jump out at you. The following dialogue is a sample of how to get and use criteria words in a selling situation:
Fran, "I appreciated your time on the telephone this morning, Mr. James. Your assistant told me that you've been having problems with the copier system and might want to investigate other possibilities."
Mr. James, "I'm not interested in buying now, although I would like to find an inexpensive solution."
Fran, "There could be an inexpensive solution, and I'd be happy to examine the possibilities even if you are not interested in buying now. May I ask you a few questions.?"

Mr. James, "What would you like to ask?"

Fran, "I'm curious. What is it that you want from your copying system? What's important about having a copying system?"

Mr. James, "Well, to make good copies when we need them."

Fran," What else?"

Mr. James, "Well, I want a system that's dependable and makes good, clear copies. We need clear copies because we have to use them in multiple presentations."

Fran, "So, you want a dependable system that makes good, clear copies. What else is really important to you?"

Mr. James, 'I want a system that's easy to use. I am tired of training new people on the machine or answering questions about how it words. I am too busy to stop every ten minutes to help with the copier. There is one thing I wish our system had. I want it to copy both sides without having to manually re-feed the paper. Is there a machine that will do that and is not very expensive?"

Fran, "Oh, yes. There are a number of ways to go that are not very expensive. By the way, what kind of budget are you working with?"

Mr. James, "I have to stay under $800.00, and I have to get a good trade-in on the equipment I'm using now."

At this point, Fran has succeeded in getting Mr. James' criteria for purchasing a new copier. The words are simple to pick out of conversation. Just as we have emphasized the words here, people emphasize their criteria when speaking by changing their tonality. Fran has already used Mr. James' criteria words. And to maximize her effectiveness, she must use them throughout her presentation and close. When Mr. James believes that the criteria, "not very expensive, dependable, easy to use, good clear copies, copy both sides without having to manually re-feed the paper, under $800.00, and a good trade-in" are met, he'll purchase a copier. By using his exact words in relation to her own product, Fran

12

matches her copiers to the criteria that motivate Mr. James to buy.

Here is an example of how she can do that:
Fran, "Mr. James, I want to put together a few possible solutions for you that are not very expensive and will give you equipment that makes good clear copies and is very dependable. I will also make sure that it is easy to use. I am sure that I can supply a machine that copies on both sides without having to re-feed the paper manually. It will take me two days to gather the information for you, so would a meeting on Thursday morning fit your schedule, sometime before lunch?"

How motivating language affects the sales cycle. As we said earlier, in a sales situation, your prospect's motivating language represents his or her criteria for purchase. Only when you and your product meet the BOS standards will you make the sale. Your clients will feel you understand their needs when you respond to them using their own words. You will build a positive atmosphere, and that will put them in the mood to hear what you have to say. This simple question, "For you, what is important about –?", gives you invaluable information about how to align yourself and your product. Work the question into the first part of your initial conversation so you can use your prospect's criteria words throughout the transaction. Use them to increase the odds of your pitch being heard favorably.

If someone has a long list of criteria, it could be time for a reality check. Can you actually satisfy this person? More than six or seven items may indicate an unrealistic customer. It could mean it is time to let the competition win one. On the other hand, if your client answers with only one very general word, it could indicate that he or she really does not know what they really want. If the person

13

responds with the criterion that it will make them happy, that does not tell you much. You need to find out the specifics of what happy looks, sounds, or feels like to them. How will the person recognize when he or she is happy? Despite the generality of "happy," it does represent the client's values in the context. We, as the service provider, must use the word "happy." At the same time, we must understand what the customer means by that word so we can give the client what he or she wants.

Here are points to remember. Too many criteria words may mean a prospect cannot be satisfied. Too few criteria words may mean the prospect has not delineated his or her needs. Find out what the customer means specifically.

Success equals learning to listen. The best way to becoming comfortable gleaning motivating language from conversation is to spend several days asking only the Motivating Words question from BOS program. Ask the question of anybody you meet, and ask it with a variety of context. The point here is to get used to hearing responses and identifying the words. Once you get a person's criteria words, use them in your conversation and carefully observe the response. Typically, people exhibit an increased interest in what you are saying. They will do this by staying in rapport with you, which means asking you questions, following your examples without interruption, continuing to engage you in conversation, or just generally showing interest.

Alternative questions. It may seem awkward to you to ask the question in exactly the formula we have given. If so, here is an alternative formula that will elicit your client's power words. "What do you really want [in an investment, car, stereo, job, or computer]? What is your motivating language?" If you answered the question at

14

the beginning of the chapter, "For you, what is important about selling?", you now know your hot-button words for the context of selling. In other words, for you to be happy in your sales situation, you must feel that the BOS criteria are being met. When other people use these words, it will get your attention.

Practice makes perfect. The idea behind motivating language is quite simple. Each of us has words and phrases that mean something unique to us, and to which we respond with increased attention. These hot-button words can change with context, just as you have different criteria for a car, a tennis partner, or a college for your kids. Gaining access to another person's criteria is as easy as asking the question, "For you, what is important about –?" See if you can pick out the customer's motivating language in the following examples.

Example 1: Mork, "What do you really want in a relationship?" Mindy, "Well, I guess I want to know that we're friends and can depend on each other in a tough situation, a person that respects you and listens to you when you need to talk. It would be great, also, if they liked the outdoors and hiking."

Example 2: Tory, "I just don't feel like eating out. Meagan, "Well, what's important about eating out?" Tory, "You mean in general, it's really good for the economy. I know that." Meagan, "No, no. I mean what is important about it for you. Tory, "Well, the regular stuff, exotic food, good selection of imported beers, no loud music, no cockroaches, and cute waitresses that pay a lot of attention to me. You know what? I don't wanna have to drive 30 miles to eat, either. It needs to be pretty close by." Megan, "How close is pretty close?" Tory, "Ten, 11 miles, 15 max."

Example 3: <u>Gifford</u>, "For you, what's really important about how accounts receivable should function?" <u>Robbins</u>, "We need to get paid faster and reduce non-payments. I'm tired of supplying distributors who are slow pay, and then go out of business. Those guys live on my credit and don't even pay for it."

Example 4: Shelby, "For you, what's really important about the investments you buy?" <u>Linda</u>, "I want something that has long-term potential and can give me a good return with no risk to my initial investment. I want security in the future, and a lump sum to live on when I'm older."

Reviewing further is essential to your learning how to distinguish motivating language from the torrent of words that come pouring out when you ask people what's important to them. We suggest that you ask this question in a variety of contexts to anyone who will let you record their answer on a recorder. At home, play their answers until you can identify their hot-button words and phrases. They will emphasize their answers with intonations just as we have emphasized the answers to these review examples.

Example 1: <u>Mindy</u>, "Well, I guess I want to know that we are friends and can depend on each other in a tough situation, a person that respects you and listens to you when you need to talk. It would be great, also, if they liked the outdoors and hiking."

Example 2: Notice the result of Meagan's failure to contextualize the question with "for you." She had to repeat the question with the proper context to get the information she wanted. <u>Tory,</u> "Well, the regular stuff, exotic food, good selection of imported beers, no loud music, no cockroaches, and cute waitresses that pay a lot of attention to me. You know what? I don't wanna have to drive 30 miles to eat, either. It needs to pretty close by."

Example 3: Robins, "We need to get paid faster and reduce non-payments. I'm tired of supplying distributors who are slow pay and then go out of business. Those guys live on my credit and don't even pay for it."

Example 4: Linda, "I want something that has long-term potential and can give me a good return with no risk to my initial investment. I want security in the future and a lump sum to live on when I'm old

Chapter 3
Enthusiasm Can Kill the Sale.

You probably have a lot of enthusiasm for what you sell. After all the sales training and pump-you-up weekends you've participated in, you'd better be enthusiastic, right? If you didn't have a big reserve of positive energy, you'd never get through all the negativity and rudeness that you run into in the sales jungle. No doubt all that installed bravado has served you well personally, but it may have turned off your clients; not all of them, mind you, but some people out there, and you have undoubtedly run into them, who possess the intuitive believe that enthusiastic people are not to be trusted. On the other hand, there are people who intuitively believe that you cannot trust anyone who isn't enthusiastic. The trick is knowing which is which and dealing with each in the way that makes them feel comfortable.

Motivating direction: For our purposes, people who appreciate enthusiasm are goal-motivated. They set an objective and work toward attaining it. At the other end of the spectrum are the BOS who detest goals. These people see problems and instinctively work to get away from them. Because of the directional nature of the two patterns involved, we call this category of the BOS program, motivating direction.

The **toward pattern**: The buzzword of toward behavior is goals. People who display this type of behavior understand goals and are motivated by them. In fact, goals motivate them to the point that they often ignore difficulties, and are certain to discount negative consequences. Toward people just don't give any energy to problems. It's the goal that matters, what gets them up in the morning and out into the day. They want to gain. They want to attain and achieve.

18

The **away from pattern:** The key word for the away from person is avoid. People with this pattern see problems. In fact, this is their great benefit. This is especially true in an organization with a lot of toward people who refuse to acknowledge what can go wrong. Away from individuals are motivated to avoid the problems they recognize. Just as problems disorient the toward person, goals trip up an away-from person. They have difficulty articulating objectives, and feel confused when given goals to accomplish. Rather than seeing the benefits goal achievement will bring they only see the problems that can arise in working toward them. Because they search out what can go wrong, away from people are valuable on a team. However, they may be labeled as party poopers and killjoys by the moving toward BOS. The away from BOS sees the moving toward BOS as risk-takers. The toward person will very likely think of the away from BOS as negative.

People can be in between. Motivating direction is a continuum. In other words, people can combine the toward and away from patterns at different degrees. In addition, there are the BOS that exhibit both patterns equally. The BOS Toward people are motivated by goals, and the Away people identify what can go wrong. As you listen to a variety of people answer this question, you will naturally distinguish the degree to which the pattern expresses in the BOS, which are not wholly toward or away from.

The question for motivating direction. The following questions reveal your motivating direction for the context of selling. Remember, the emphasized part of the question is the formula. The context is the part you would modify by filling in your product or service.

19

(1), What do you want from selling? (2), What will having that really do for you? The answer to the first question will consist of criteria words, typically the same ones depending on the context you elicited by the motivating language question. It's important to remember the BOS words and phrases because you ask the second question by inserting them into the formula. For example, if you answered the first question, "What do you want from selling?" With more money, the second would be phrased, "What will having more money do for you?" the information that tells you whether someone is toward or away from, comes from the second question. If you don't get a clear reading of your client's motivational compass, keep asking the question inserting the last answer you got until you feel you're clear on what having the criteria things will do for the person. Will it add to their life in some way, or will help them avoid something? Are they attracted or repelled?

How to interpret what you hear. We lace our conversation with our motivating direction. Toward people answer the question with things they hope to achieve or gain. If you ask them what having a good job will do for them, they will say things like, "It will pay for a new car," or, "I can meet new people that are more like me," or, "It will buy me the time to spend with my Family.

A toward person talks about how attaining goals will benefit life. These people can label what their goals will give them. An away from person won't do that. Away from speech contains things to be avoided, and answer the question regarding a job, they'll say things like, "It keeps me from getting evicted " or, "It gives me security," or, "It keeps me off the streets." A person who uses the phase "keep from," is almost certainly away from.

Here is what Mr. James, the man who was looking for an inexpensive copier might sound like as an away from.
Fran, "Mr. James, what will having a copying system that is dependable, makes good clear copies, is easy to use, and is not expensive really do for you?" Notice that Fran has inserted Mr. James' criteria words into the formula.
Mr. James, "What do you mean what will it do for me?"
Fran, "What will it really do for you."
Mr. James, "Well, I guess it will keep me from being so frustrated when I need copies and can't finish a project."

Clearly, Mr. James has identified a problem in this copier situation. It's costing him time and frustration. But notice, also, that he doesn't really answer the question because he asks for classification. An away from doesn't conceive of the world as doing anything for him. To sell Mr. James, Fran will have to help him avoid his problem; either by solving it or by helping him dodge it.

Now let's listen to the speech pattern of a toward Mr. James as he answers the same question.
Mr. James, "Well, I guess I'll be able to accomplish a lot more work and take on some other projects. Clearly, Mr. James is thinking about how a new copier will enhance his position. He's not aiming to avoid unpleasant consequences.

Let's look at an away from pattern in another context.
Allen, "Steve, you talked about wanting to have an investment that is safe and still gives you a return that would stay ahead of inflation. What would having that kind of investment really do for you?"
Steve, "Well, if you could find something like that, I could relax knowing that my savings would not lose its buying power when I retired." Obviously, Steve is an away from investor. He wants to be sure he keeps his savings from losing their value. He indicates no interest in maximizing

21

his return or seeking out high yields. He wants to avoid losing money.

Here's how a toward investor would answer the same question.
Sarah, "It will give me an opportunity to grow my excess cash flow into something that will let me travel and really enjoy my retirement." Sarah's answer is completely different. She talks about opportunity and growth, and identifies options that are exciting to her. Travel and enjoyment certainly add to her life. They are not something she's trying to avoid. She doesn't entertain any of the worry we heard in Steve's answer. Sarah simply isn't focused on what can go wrong.

How motivating direction affects the sales cycle. As you can imagine, a mismatch in motivating direction can create a lot of problems for a salesperson. A goal-motivated salesperson will get nowhere with a client who only sees what can go wrong getting there. It's unlikely that he or she will build a rapport necessary to consummate a deal. The away from buyer will continually pick apart the gains and benefits the toward salesperson identifies. Have you ever had a customer like that?

Or consider the away from saleswoman who insists on pointing out the client's current problems to show how the product solves them. Unfortunately, the toward client needs to hear how he or she benefits from the purchase. To be motivated to buy, he or she must be convinced that something is to be gained. Avoiding problems does not motivate this prospect. Matching your client's motivating direction is a very important step in building rapport. If you're not going in the same direction, you'll not get to the checkbook at the same time. When you match their picture of the world, they sense that you innately understand. They will trust you. Failing to match in his category creates an uneasy feeling that you're out of synch with your customer.

Let's take a look at how Allen handled his toward and away from customers. This is the toward customer. Allen, "Sarah, when your money is invested, you can begin examining even more possibilities of how to spend your retirement years. You can even begin doing the travel right now." Allen knows that Sarah needs something to aim for, something that she believes will improve her retirement. By relating that future goal to the current moment, he enlivens the goal in a way that is more compelling than leaving it in some vague future.

Allen's approach with the away from Steve has to be different. Here is how he phrases his response. Allen, "With your money safely invested in this program, you can rest easy knowing that you won't be losing your equity to inflation." When closing away from buyers, it is crucial to reassure them that they will avoid the problems they have identified. Since they want to be kept from the difficulties, it's important to tell them that the problem won't be a problem if they use your product or service. The form of the communication is, "I want to keep from having this happen," to which you answer, "You won't have that problem if you give us the business."

You cannot dismiss the problem and concentrate on what they may attain, gain, or achieve, because that does nothing to ease their instinct that something can go wrong. To master this part of the BOS program, do the review that follows, and then spend several days asking only these two questions of as many people as possible. "What do you want from __? What will having that do for you?" Listen closely to the answers, and before long, you'll be able to identify each pattern easily and consistently. Practice matching each speech pattern and observed the effects on rapport when you match or mismatch. At first, you may feel awkward outside your own pattern, but that will change as you see how quickly people response to your matching speech.

What is your motivating direction? Now, evaluate your own answers to the questions, "What do you want from selling?" and, "What will having that do for you?" Are you a goal-oriented toward achiever, or are you a problem-spotting away from avoider? Do you want to attain and gain, or do you want to steer clear and get rid of? If you can't quite decide, keep asking yourself the second question, "What will having that –?" the criteria you used to answer the first question – "do for me?"

Practice makes perfect. The patterns of the motivating direction category are easy to spot. Does the person answer with benefits or problems? Pick out the patterns in these examples.

Example 1: Myrna, "What will having a relationship like the one you want really do for you?" Carla, "It will keep me from having to worry about having someone to grow old with."

Example 2: Brian, "What will having the kind of investment you what really do for you?" Linda, "I'll be able to plan for the future and reach my goals."

Example 3: Peter, "What will having that kind of investment really do for you?" Paul, "I can get old without worrying, and I can have the cash to have some fun."

Example 4: Lisa, "What will having that kind of class you want really do for you?" Paul, "That's easy. It would keep me up on all the recent developments in optics so I could stay on my career track and keep the bill collectors away from my door."

Reviewing further is essential to learning how to distinguish the patterns in motivating direction. We suggest that you ask this question in a variety of contexts of anyone who will let you record their answer on a recorder. At home, play their answers until you are sure whether they are giving you a benefit, a problem, or a combination of the two. Do they relate to goals or to what can go wrong? Where is their focus?

Answers to the review

Example 1: Myrna, "what will having a relationship like the one you want really do for you?" Carla, "It will keep me from having to worry about having someone to grow old with." Carla is away from in relationships. She wants to avoid worrying.

Example 2: Brian, "What will having the kind of investment you what really do for you?" Linda, "I'll be able to plan for the future and reach my goals." Linda is a toward investor. She understands goals.

Example 3: Peter, "What will having the kind of investment you want really do for you?" Paul, "I can get old without worrying, and I can have the cash to have some fun." Paul is a mixed pattern investor, what we call equally toward and away from. He wants to avoid worrying and he wants to have fun.

Example 4: Lisa, "What will having kind of class you want really do for you?" Eric, "That's easy. It would keep me up on all the recent developments in optics so I could stay on my career track and keep the bill collectors away from my door." Eric is also a mixed pattern, what we called more toward than away from. He answers with two toward patterns and one away from. He understands goals, career track, and he sees how a class could benefit him, "keep me up on," but he also wants to avoid the bill collectors. In responding to him, focus on toward languages and speech patterns, but be sure to address any problems he identifies.

Chapter 4
Who Really Tells Your Customer to Say Yes?

Do you have a friend or know someone who is really hard-headed and refuses to take input from you or anyone else? It's as if no opinion but their own has any validity. It's also likely that you've come across that person's opposite, the man or woman who seems to have no opinion of his or her own, and will follow your lead wherever it goes.

Motivating source: These two patterns represent the poles on a continuum of behavior that makes up a basic part of the BOS program the source of a person's motivation. Are they motivated by circumstances outside themselves or within? Motivating source reaches far into our behavior. This part of the human operation system measures whether a person values input from others or makes decisions independently. We have labeled the patterns, but make it up as external and internal.

Recently, a client called Marvin asking him to accompany a key salesperson on a major presentation. The client explained that this one order was worth several million dollars to the company and the company wanted him to observe the meeting and provide feedback to the sale executive and the organization. He was introduced as part of a reengineering team that was evaluating manufacturing processes in human applications and he sat inconspicuously to the customer's right, and off to the side. The salesman launched into his presentation and Marvin immediately noticed that he continually referred to himself and his decision about how good the product was and how it fit very well into the customer's needs. Several times he either said or implied how important he felt it was that the customer do exactly what the salesman wanted, which basically was to buy the product.

Every time the sales executive talked about what he thought, Marvin observed that the customer's facial muscles tightened, which is a clear indication that the man was not aligned with the sales representative's language. To Marvin, this indicated that the customer was internal, and did not want to be given directions. Intuitively, the sales executive felt his client's attention slipping away, and instinctively pressed harder. Finally, in frustration, the customer turned to Marvin and said, "Well, you're the reengineering expert. What do you think about what Bill is saying about how your products could fit into our future growth plans?"

Of course, Marvin knew next to nothing about the technology that was being pitched, but he did understand that the sales executive had lost rapport with the client. If the sale were to be salvaged, he would have to reestablish good will. So he said that the information that had already been presented was only information that he, the customer, could examine and determine whether it was appropriate for the future growth of the company. "You're the only person who can make that decision. So whatever I say will just be added information," Marvin concluded. Immediately, he noticed the customer's cheek muscles relax, and he smiled as he said, "That's exactly right. I am the only person that could make that decision."

As the conversation continued, the man turned his chair toward Marvin and began talking to him instead of the salesperson. After a few minutes, he stood up and asked if Marvin would like to go to the cafeteria, have a cup of coffee, and talk in a more relaxed environment while the sales executive met with the engineering manager to work out the specifics of the product integration. Marvin and the president had a great cup a coffee, a good conversation, and the sale was made.

This story points out how important it is to determine whether an individual's motivating source is internal or external. In this case, the president of the company sorted internally, which meant that he was the person who could make the decision. It also meant that he would subconsciously resist anyone telling him what he should do. The merest suggestion that someone else's input is required breaks rapport with an internal. The president aligned with Marvin because he presented a language pattern that aligned with the way the man's brain sorted for a motivating source.

When Marvin said that only he could make that decision, he felt instinctively that Marvin understood him. It's a complex world out there. Some people won't ever do what you tell them to do, and others won't do anything unless you tell them to. The trick is knowing how to tell one from the other, and you're about to find out exactly how that's done.

The **external pattern.** A person with the external pattern relies on the evaluations and judgments of other people to know whether he's done a good job. In forming opinions, externals depend on criteria and judgments outside themselves. They readily conform to other people's beliefs and measure themselves by the criteria of others, particularly the BOS of their supervisors, customers, and friends. In a sales situation, they depend on what others decide. What motivates them to make a decision comes from what other people say.

The **internal pattern**. Persons with the internal pattern do accept direction from other people. In forming their opinions, they will take outside input and evaluate it against their personal value systems. They're perfectly capable and willing to evaluate their own performance by their own standards, no matter where they are in the corporate hierarchy. Criteria set by another person are irrelevant when evaluating their own performance. In the world of the internal, only their own opinion really matters.

Internal and external represent the two poles of a continuum of behavior. As with any continuum, few people are going to be completely internal or external. But one or the other pattern will predominate in a given context. Your clients will continually use speech patterns that demonstrate whether they rely on their own criteria or the judgments of others in making decisions. This feature of the BOS program determines the influencing language that will be most effective. With the internal, you will acknowledge that it is a decision they have to make on their own, and do your best not to insert your opinion into the process. On the other hand, with externals you can freely give input because they will feel lost without it.

The question for motivating source. Your answer to the following question reveals your motivating source. Please answer it for yourself. How do you know that you've done a good job? The answer to this question demonstrates the source of your motivation in the context of your job. Do you need input from others or are your opinions sufficient? In the next section, you'll learn how to spot the speech patterns that indicate internal and external motivating source.

How to interpret what you hear. Dialogue A. Joan, salesperson, "Jim, we've talked about the kinds of investments you want and what they'll really do for you. I'm wondering, in the past, when you made decisions about investing, how did you know that you made a good decision at the time you made it?" Jim, "I guess I just kind of felt it inside. Joan, when you make a decision, you just know when it's right."

Dialogue B. Joan, "Terry, we've talked about the kinds of investments you want and what they'll really do for you. I'm wondering, in the past, when you made decisions about investing, how did you know that you made a good decision at the time you made it?" Terry, "I listened to the feedback of my accountant my two partners. If they said it looked like a good deal, well, with that kind of endorsement, I just felt I had to take the risk. And, I was glad I did. It turned out to be a great investment."

What do you notice in the answers of Joan's two prospects? Jim and Terry have very different responses to her question. Jim responses in typical internal fashion; he just knows. Internals will use phrases like, "I know," and, "personal satisfaction." They will often have a list of criteria that constitutes the measure of how they know something is good. "I know it's good because –"

Terry uses feedback to decide. He solicits and listens to the opinions of others before he acts. The content of external's answer to this question refers to other people or the criteria of other people. There is no emphasis on person satisfaction or some hazy, almost mystical, "I just know." They know because someone tells them.

More than any speech pattern the particular language, content is the evidence of an external in the BOS program. There are other people involved in the answer?

How the motivating source affects the sales cycle. A person's motivating source dictates the kind of close you will use. For instance, do you think testimonials are effective with internal customers? They couldn't care less what someone else thinks about your product. They will make up their minds without benefit of your opinion, thank you very much. On the other hand, an external will relish what others have to say.

This is how Joan responded to Jim, the internal prospect. Joan, "I understand what you're saying, Jim. Well, we've talked about the Ajax fund and how it meets your particular needs. You have all the data and only you can make the decision to get in the program today. How do you want to handle this?" Notice how Joan leaves the decision completely with him Jim.

Now observe how she changes this close when she talked to Terry, the external. Joan, "I understand what you're saying, Terry. We've talked about the Ajax fund and how it meets your particular needs. Many of my clients who have wanted similar returns and ability have been very happy in the fund. You have all the data and have examined it. Based on what you've told me, Terry, this is the foundation investment fund for you. Let's finish this receipt form so you can join a group of satisfied clients.

With Terry, Joan inserts herself more clearly into the process, externalizing the criteria. She also stresses the satisfaction of others involved in the program; something would be completely wasted on Jim or internal. You will certainly encounter people who mix internal and external language patterns. When they answer the question, note the first pattern they use and emphasize that in your presentation. Follow up with the other pattern. If they mix patterns, mix your language appropriately.

We have found that people sometimes interpret motivating source prematurely. Here's an example of misreading the motivating source. A participant in one of our seminars related this story. She had evaluated one of her clients, a CEO as an external because he had to get his operating officer's feedback before making a decision. Despite her evaluation, she could not influence him by using example response language. She did manage to get the second measurement of the operating officer, and she saw that her judgment had been premature. The CEO did ask for the man's opinion, but he clearly evaluated his response against his own criteria. He made decisions internally. With that information, she changed her language to that of internal, removing herself and her criteria from the table, and closed the sale.

"I sold the engagement because I changed my language pattern to match his motivating source," she said. "I gave the whole decision over to him, and he decided. That's what internals do best."

We suggest that you spend several days just asking this one question of as many people as you can. With only a little practice, you will quickly develop the ability to hear and evaluate the clues to a person's motivating source. After you have deciphered that pattern, match it by giving them the appropriate cues. Then intentionally mismatch and observe any changes in the quality of the interaction.

Alternative questions. How do you know that you have made a good decision at the time you made it? How do you know you have seen a good movie? How do you know a restaurant is good? What is your motivating source? How did you answer the question, "How do you know that you've done a good job?" Did your answer have the mysterious, "I just know," pattern, or do they rely on just outside input to make decisions?

Practice makes perfect. The internal/external patterns of the motivating source category are easy to spot. Does the person make the decision within himself or herself or do they allow other people to make the decision for them?

Example 1: <u>Myrna</u>, "How did you know that you made a good decision on the last car you bought at the time you bought it?" <u>Carla</u>, "I felt it the moment I sat in the driver's seat. It was definitely right for me."

Example 2: <u>Brian</u>, "How did you know that you made a good decision on the last car you bought at the time you bought it?" <u>Linda</u>, "After all the research and driving around I had to go with what salesman was telling me. He's in the business, after all, and should know what he's talking about."

Example 3: <u>Peter</u>, "How did you know you did a good job on that last project?" <u>Paul,</u> "Well, everyone I talked to told me what a great job I did. Plus, I felt good about the way things had happened."

Example 4: <u>Lisa</u>, "How did you know you did a good job on that last project?" <u>Laura</u>, I just knew it. It seemed to me the results were obvious."

Reviewing further is essential learning how to distinguish the patterns in motivating source. We suggest that you answer this question in a variety of contexts of anyone who will let you record their answer. At home, play their answers until you're sure whether they make decisions internally or need input from other people.

Answers to the review.

Example 1: <u>Myrna</u>, "How did you know that you made a good decision on the last car you bought at the time you bought it?" <u>Carla</u>, "I felt it the moment I sat in the driver's seat. It was definitely right for me." Carla is an internal. She knew when her criteria were met.

Example 2: Brian, "How did you know that you made a good decision on the last car you bought at the time you bought it?" Linda, "After all the research and driving around I had to go with what salesman was telling me. He's in the business, after all, and should know what he's talking about." Linda is an external. She values the salesperson's opinion over her own.

Example 3: Peter, "How did you know you did a good job on that last project?" Paul, "Well, everyone I talked to told me what a great job I did. Plus, I felt good about the way things had happened." Paul is a mixed pattern, equally internal and external. He takes into account the opinions of others, but he also knows within himself.

Example 4: Lisa, "How did you know you did a good job on that last project?" Laura, I just knew it. It seemed to me the results were obvious." Laura is internal. I, me, and nobody else.

Here is a quick review of Chapters 1-4:

This is an opportunity for you to practice evaluating speech patterns found thus far in the book.

We will eavesdrop on the conversation of Tim Jacobs, a business consultant, and Riley Miller, the CEO of a small manufacturing company.

Jacobs wants to use the BOS information to help him get a consulting contract. Every few chapters throughout this book, we will drop in on their conversation. In this installment, the two men have just met after they were networked together by a mutual friend. This conversation will serve as the foundation for Jacobs' knowledge of what the customer wants and how to best serve him. Your assignment is to pick out Miller's motivating language and his BOS patterns for motivating direction and motivating source. Is he toward or away from? Is he internal or external? What are his hot button words?

Miller, "Good morning. Come into my office. Let's find out why Allen thought we should meet." Jacobs, "I appreciate your time and I'm anxious to learn more about your company." Miller, "I really don't have much time this morning. I have another meeting in 30 minutes." Jacobs, "Sounds like you're pretty busy. Allen said that you needed some consulting work, so I'm wondering what kind of consulting work you really want." Miller, "Well, the truth is, I'm having a hell of a delay in my accounts receivable and I'm suspicious that we're not handling that function very well. I'm sure there's room for improvement."

Jacobs, "Regarding your accounts receivable, for you, what's important about how it should function?" Miller, "We have to get paid faster and reduce non-payments. I'm tired of supplying distributors who are slow pay and then go out of business. These guys are living on my credit and not even paying for it." Jacobs, "I've had the opportunity to help a number of manufacturers with similar needs. In this area of our business, we've developed functions that identify distributors that are potentially slow pay and are not financially sound. Those are the ones that usually go out of business after they receive your products. The functions we've developed also help get money in faster."

Miller, "That sounds very interesting. What would it cost for us to use you?" Jacobs, "That depends on a number of things. For instance, I would need to know how your functions are organized now. I would need to evaluate the systems you have that support those functions. And I would have to hear more about the results you want to achieve. If you had the kind of accounts receivable function that gave you the things you

36

wanted, what would that really do for you and your and company?" Miller, "Well, it would keep me from losing money and wasting time with deadbeats. The only way we can grow is to have cash flow moving and spending time getting more and better customers. Without that, we aren't going to be around for my kids to benefit."

Jacobs, "I can appreciate what you're saying. It's the same in my business. If we don't have the supporting business functions to protect us from fast-talking deadbeats, we can't get better, and we can sure lose what we've been working for. That's not lesson we want to teach our kids." Miller, "You've got that right. How long would it take for you to examine our present functions and tell me what you can do and give me an estimate of what it will cost?" Jacobs, "If I could spend a full day with your accounts receivable people, and some more time with you, I'll have enough information to prepare a bid that outlines my services and the cost. Have you ever used a consulting service before?" Miller, "Yes, once, when we were seeing up an assembly facility." Jacobs, "I'm curious. When you hired the consultants, how did you know that you hired the right group?" Miller, "I don't think I've ever been asked that before. It's good question. I listened to their pitches and I checked their references. After I examined all the inputs, I had a clear sense of who would do the best job."

Jacobs, "I'm impressed that you're so thorough when making these kinds of decisions. You definitely don't want to make a mistake when it comes to your accounts receivable. I'll certainly supply you with names and phones numbers of past clients so you can confirm my competence. They can tell you the results of my services. I'll be happy to supply you with any other information you might need. But I recognize that only you can make this decision." Miller, "I want you to know that I'm evaluating another organization and I'll be comparing your proposal to theirs."

Jacobs, "It's good that you're making comparisons. I would be able to schedule time next week to spend here. What would be the best time for you so that we can get the information I need to develop a proposal?" Miller, "The middle of the week. But I need to check with my accounts receivable manager first and then confirm a time." Jacobs, "Great. I know that time is important. So once my information gathering is complete, I'll be able to help you be paid faster and identify those deadbeats before you waste your time or money. I noticed that we're getting close to your next appointment." Miller, "That's true. Call me this afternoon to set up a schedule for next week." Jacobs, "Good. Thanks for your time. I'll call this afternoon."

Answers to the review.
Motivating language. Mr. Miller's criteria words for the accounts receivable function are, "paid faster, reduce non-payments," and, "slow pay."

Motivating direction. He is a mixed pattern, more away from than toward. He spotted two problems, losing money and saving time, and stated them first. But he also sees a goal of growing a business for his kids to benefit from.

Motivating source. He is an internal. Although he takes input from other sources, he clearly makes the decision using his own internal

Chapter 5
Not Being Creative Can Make You Money.

Imagine that it's Christmas morning and you've drawn the task of putting together a complicated toy. What do you do once the box is open and pieces are out where you can work with them? Do you take a look at the picture on the box and start fitting pieces together, or do you open the instructions and start at Step 1? Or let's say the toy gave you the Japanese instructions, or left them out completely. How would you respond? Would you attempt to put the toy together anyway, or would you move on to some other Christmas chore?

The process approach.
Your reaction to this situation tells a lot about you. It reveals the process approach of your BOS program. It describes your operating method. Do you look for procedures to follow, or do you seek out new opportunities? We've labeled the patterns elicited by this question as options and procedures.

The options pattern. A completely options person wants to expand his possibilities. You may have met people like this. They're the ones who see the opportunity in every situation. They evaluate everything in terms of their criteria and whether it offers them the opportunity to satisfy those criteria. Rules and procedures stymie options people, although they are quite good at developing those same rule and procedures. The options person creates a process as a solution, not a rule to live by. He or she abhors routine and often stretches the limits, like getting to work on time. Watch your coworkers; those who consistently come in a few minutes late will almost always turn out to be options. They are the people who read instructions only as a last resort, and only then because it's just another option for them to try.

The procedures pattern. On the other end of the spectrum a procedures person feels obliged to follow the rules, to do things in an orderly procedure. He or she feels comfortable as long as there's a system to deal with the situation. This person lives for step-by-step instructions and without them is lost. Procedures people never proceed without reading the instructions. Ironically, as much as they love the step-by-step, they're lousy at making them up. Without a procedure for dealing with things, they become discombobulated, and stressed until they get an outlined way of proceeding. Routine is their greatest comfort.

The question for process approach.
The following question reveals your process approach for the context of being a salesperson. Please answer it for yourself. Why did you choose to be a sales professional?

How to interpret what you hear.
Your client's answer to this question will tell you much about them. Do they look for opportunities or do they follow sequences? Do they like routines or abhor them? Will they need the assurance that there's an orderly procedure to your interaction? Through the following sample dialogues, you will begin to recognize these two speech patterns and understand just how easy they are to distinguish from each other.

Dialogue A. Allen, salesperson, "I was pleased when we were able to schedule this meeting, Sarah. You may be wondering how our services can do what we say they can. Many of our clients have had similar thoughts before we met. I am curious, Sarah. Why did you choose to use an outside vendor for this project?" Sarah, the client, "Well, Allen, about a year ago, the president asked me to head up a project that would deliver a fully integrated information system that could coordinate manufacturing, sales, marketing, and finance into one process. We started with the needs of each department and then examined the correlating aspects of their needs. After identifying needs and purpose, I identified what talents we had internally. Finally, we determined that to complete a project

40

like this, we would either have to hire more talent, or go outside on a contract basis. That brings us to this stage of the process."

Dialogue B. Allen, "I was pleased when we were able to schedule this meeting, Susan. You may be wondering how our services can do what we say they can. Many of our clients have had similar thoughts before we met. I am curious, Susan. Why did you choose to use an outside vendor for this project?"
Susan, "Well, Allen, we need a fully integrated system that will coordinate all our departments' activities. We need to cut costs and upgrade our processes to a state-of-the-art system. We don't have the talent internally, so we decided to go outside for help."
What do you notice about these two responses? There are BOS clues everywhere. In Dialogue A, Sarah tells a story. She outlines the procedure her company went through in making their decision. She's focused on methods, steps, and sequence in time. A specific step goes first, then a second, and so forth. She answers a why question with facts, "one year, president's request, coordinating manufacturing, sales, marketing, and finance." Then comes the step-by-step breakdown that's so important to the procedures individual. Actually, Sarah answered the question, "How did you choose," not "why." When she finishes, you know she makes decisions, even if you don't know the criteria those decisions are based on.

In answering the question, "Why did you choose?" a person who describes a process is demonstrating the procedures pattern. The process is important to them.

Susan, in Dialogue B, does not give any facts in her answer. She answers the why question with needs and reasons. The response is filled with her criteria for purchase, "fully integrated, coordinated departments, cutting costs and upgrading." You only get a hint of the process they went through in deciding to use an outside vendor. Her answer has no story to it, no people or events or timetables, just criteria that

41

need to be met. Because of that emphasis, her BOS process approach is options.

A few months ago, Marvin arranged to meet a potential client at a restaurant. After an initial introduction, Marvin noticed that when asked by the maître d' whether he had a preference of seating, the client immediately responded, "Well, first I want to make sure that we're away from a high-traffic area. In addition, I always sit by a window. And, of course, I want to be in a non-smoking area." Marvin closely observed the process with which the man made the decision of where to sit, and decided that he was initially sorting for procedures, followed by particular criteria or options backup. To break this down for you, he started with, "First, I want to make sure that we're away from," followed by a procedure of how he would choose a seat, and concluded with specific reasons.

Working on the assumption that he had a procedures pattern, Marvin went on to develop an excellent relationship with this person. He began the conversation by setting up a procedure to follow through lunch and the business discussion. It worked quite well. The man felt comfortable during their conversation and totally aligned with Marvin's presentation. By the end of lunch, he was no longer a potential client. They were doing business together.

Sometimes you do not have to ask the question. All you have to do is observe how an individual response when interacting with another person. All of us constantly demonstrate the traits catalogued in the BOS program. It is simply a matter of paying attention to the cues. Nonetheless, it is always a good idea to back up your observation by asking the question for that context.

How process approach affects the sales cycle. You will use this component of the BOS to affect how you structure your presentation and you close the sale. With an options customer, you can bounce around, talking about the many ways your product or service will expand their possibilities. You will certainly stress flexibility and use their criteria words.

If your customer is a procedures person, your presentation had better be well organized and methodical. It always helps to put forward an outline of the whole presentation beforehand. Then be sure to do it in just that order. Remember, step by step makes procedures people feel comfortable. A big advantage of outlining the process is that a procedures person needs to complete that process. This person won't abandoned ship mid-process and go with the next opportunity presented. Procedures people tend to distrust options people, something you need to be aware of if you're an options person selling to a procedures customer. On the other hand, options think of procedures as dull and inflexible. If you're having that feeling about your client, modify your approach by breaking your presentation into steps.

Pre-closing Sarah, the procedures buyer.
Remember, procedures people distrust those who bring them unstructured presentations of materials. For them, interactions must have a beginning, middle, and end. With a client like Sarah, you must either fit into her sequence, or create one for her to follow. For procedures customers, the primary considerations are identifying the process and completing it. If they seem to waiver, respond by breaking things down into steps. You might explain the process of getting it from the plant to their door, for instance. Whatever you do, don't give them new options such as more benefits for their comparison. Expensive possibilities might excite you, but procedures people operate most effectively within known procedures. They become lost without a planned course of action. As we said, they follow the rules and instinctively distrust anyone who does not.

Here's how Allen responded to Sarah's description of their vendor selection process. Allen, "That sounds like a very logical way to make a decision. Before I get started with my presentation, I want to outline what I am going to do. First, I'll go over your specific needs. Second, I will explain how our services work and the types of projects that we have completed. The third step will be the integration of how we would handle your projects and additional value added benefits. Fourth, All your questions will be addressed and any additional information you need will be provided. And, finally, our fees will be agreed on according to your budget requirements so that an agreement can be authorized. Oh, I almost forgot, it is my procedure to take you to lunch a few days before we begin in order to celebrate our agreement, and to ensure that we're on track. By the way, what kind of food do you like to eat?" Sarah, "I like to eat healthy. So something light would be my preference." Allen, "Great. I know an excellent place. Well, Sarah, let's get started."

I emphasized the steps so you could see how easy it is to procedurize things. You do not need to emphasize the steps with your voice. The customer's response to them is unconscious.

Preselling Susan, options buyer.
Listen closely to the words and phrases the options person uses. In answering your why question, she's telling you her criteria words. They may even be the same words used to answer the motivating language question in Chapter 2. Those words represent her values, what she is looking for. And, you must match them if you want to make the sale. Whatever else you do, remember those words.

An options person will explain her choices in terms of opportunities, to learn, to make money, to improve, to get a free meal, to meet someone new, or to upgrade the system. Options people are motivated to expand their horizons, so they respond when benefits are couched as possibilities. Given a choice between following procedures and exploring new territory, they will always choose to explore. You should talk to them about why your product is better. Use their criteria words often. Never discuss how with them. Procedures limit them and they do not respond to limitations. For example, the instant you start to talk about the process of filling the order, the contracts, the shippers, the bills of lading, the nuts and bolts of making it work, they lose interest and you lose the deal. Here is Allen's response to Susan's list of criteria words.

Allen, "Good. It is sounds as if you have a number of activities to satisfy. It is our practice to provide enough options for our clients so they can go in a number of directions to meet their goals. The results of our services can provide you with a track to follow that include many feeder lines, so to speak. You're going to have choices, so the real challenges of this project aren't missed." As with any continuum of behavior, few people are going to be wholly options or procedures. But, for the most part, one or the other pattern will predominate. Your clients will continually demonstrate their preferred patterns through speech cues that will become as obvious to you as the noses on their faces once you are used to listening for them. When you have delineated their patterns adjust your presentation accordingly.

Here is a hint. An easy way to remember the distinction between options and procedures is to think of instructions. When putting something together, and options person dives in and only reads the instruction once he or she has failed at least once to put it together. A procedure person will not begin the project without reading the instructions. If no instructions are available, they will not attempt to put it together.

Spend a few days asking only this question from the BOS profile. This is the best way to learn to evaluate the responses. It won't take many examples of each pattern before you can quickly distinguish between them.

What is your process approach? Where do you fall on the spectrum between options and procedures? Did you answer a how question or why? Did you outline a scenario with facts? "I answered an ad, interviewed, trained, and got the job." Or did you describe the opportunities your current job offers. "It was a golden opportunity to increase my income, to work with people I liked." Did you step through a procedure or did you reel off a criterion?

Practice makes perfect. The patterns for a process approach are simple to decipher. Does the person answer with criteria or facts? Do they answer a how question or a why? Pick out the patterns in these examples.

Example 1: Allen, "Sarah you really like the car you bought last year. I'm wondering, why did you choose that particular model?" Sarah "It really looked great and the price was right."

Example 2: Allen, "Jim, I can tell you really like your new car. I was wondering, why did you choose that particular model?" Jim, "Last year when I was looking for a car, I must have visited ten different dealerships. I collected lots of information, but it came down to two sporty models at two different dealers. The decisive factor came when the sales manager showed me his numbers compared to the other dealer. When that happened, it seemed right to make a decision."

Example 3: Carla, "Buying a home is a decision that will have lasting effects. We talked about the last home you purchased, and I'm curious about why you chose to buy that one." Michelle, "As I told you earlier, the reason was that it fit our pocketbook, and it was in a location that had good schools for the kids. It was also important that the commute to work was convenient for both my husband and me."

Example 4: Carla, "Buying a home is a decision that will have lasting effects. We talked about the last home you purchased,

46

and I'm curious about why you chose to buy that one." <u>Tom</u>, "It's really a long story. It started about eight months before. My wife and I saw the house being built. We lived on the side of town and wanted to move to that area. We stopped to talk with the builder and he kept our name. About six months later, the builder called and told us that the people he'd been building it for couldn't close. We put a contract on it immediately."

Reviewing further is essential in learning how to distinguish the patterns in process approach. We suggest that you ask this question in a variety of contexts of people who will let you record their answers. At home, play their answers until you're sure whether they give you criteria or tell you the procedure they went through to arrive at their decision.

Here are answers to review.

Example 1: <u>Sarah</u> "It really looked great and the price was right." Options. She answers with her criteria for purchase.

Example 2: <u>Jim</u>, "Last year when I was looking for a car, I must have visited ten different dealerships. I collected lots of information, but it came down to two sporty models at two different dealers. The clincher came when the sales manager showed me his numbers compared to the other dealer. When that happened, it seemed right to make a decision." Jim is procedures because he answers with a story that tells how he made his decision.

Example 3: <u>Michelle</u>, "As I told you earlier, the reason was that it fit our pocketbook, and it was in a location that had good schools for the kids. It was also important that the commute to work was convenient for both my husband and me." Michelle is options because she tells us what's important to her about the house she bought.

Example 4: <u>Tom,</u> "It's really a long story. It started about eight months before. My wife and I saw the house being built. We lived on the side of town and wanted to move to that area. We stopped to talk with the builder and he kept our name. About six months later, the builder called and told us that the people he'd been building it for couldn't close. We put a contract on it immediately." Tom is procedures because he tells a story that begins at the beginning, and then moves sequentially through time to a conclusion. He does throw in one phrase of criteria, and that is that he and his wife wanted to move to that area.

Chapter 6
Talking Your Way Out of Sales

A friend who owns a printing company related this story. He was awaiting a government contract for $3 million to $4 million in business. In order to obtain this contract, a government inspector had to come by his plant to review a production sample. The inspector arrived about mid-day and they decided to have lunch before looking at the samples. Right after lunch, the printing company owner and the inspector went into a gift shop near where they ate in Fort Worth, Texas, which is known in the Lone Star state as Cowtown.

The inspector wanted to buy his son a cowboy belt to take back to Washington DC. While in the gift shop, our friend was able to observe the inspector's decision strategy. The man went to a belt rack and removed a belt. He looked at the inside and on the outside, put it back, and pulled a second belt. He scrutinized that belt intently, examining all the seam work, put it back, and pulled a third belt from the rack. He looked closely at the stitching and the craftsmanship. Then went to the counter and purchased that belt.

By observing that behavior, my printer friend determined that the inspector from Washington DC made decisions visually. When they returned to his plant for the inspection, the owner took great pains to show the inspector all the detail of the printing process. He pointed out the craftsmanship in the color mixing of the pictures and presented his product in a very visual manner. I will finish this story in the next chapter on convincer strategy, but I wanted to use it here to illustrate it is important to notice how people make decisions. By the way, they did sign a contract that day for the printing project.

Decision strategy.
Just as a DOS program orients the computer to accept data through the keyboard, an optical scanner, or a disk, so your

individual BOS program orients your brain to take in data through your eyes, ears, or feelings. Every person has a decision strategy. They ring one sensory channel over the other two. We call this decision strategy because it's crucial to how we decide everything. Yet basic as this is to the way we act, react, and interact, few people know how to decipher it consistently. Knowing a person's decision strategy is a potent piece of data in creating relationships. It allows us to give others information in the way they are predisposed to receiving it.

The possible patterns are visual, auditory, and feelings. Some people prefer to call feelings kinesthetic.

Visual. As you would expect, visual people primarily learn and are convinced by seeing things done. They prefer to take in information by observing. They are most at home with pictures, graphs, and other forms of visual data. They tend to ignore or delete much of the information present in other ways. Hand them a brochure while you're speaking, and their attention will go immediately to paper and you will have lost them to what you're saying.
People with a visual pattern may like to read information as well as see images. The desire to read demonstrates a visual preference. Many people you meet, about 70 percent, will be visually oriented, just because visual stimulation begins at such an early age. The television has influenced many decision strategy patterns.

Auditory. Auditory people listen and tend to ignore or delete information that is not spoken. Hand an auditory a sheet of paper while you're talking and he won't even glance at it. This decision strategy is found in approximately 25 percent of the population.

Feelings. Feelings people are hands-on and must do a task to learn it. They value the experience of doing it over seeing it done, or hearing about it. In fact, they often disregard information presented in those ways. Feelings people comprise the remaining 5 percent of the population. In addition to these three categories, there is some mixing. There are people who are both visual and auditory, others who are auditory and feelings, others, feelings and visual. Even in cases of combined preferences, however, one sensory system is typically preferred over the other.

We want to make it clear that it's not that a visual person cannot hear, rather they are over-sighted. They simply depend more on visual cues and stimulation than other forms of communication. The same is true for auditory and feelings people. Think about how people learn in a school context. Some are perfectly happy with a pure lecture format, auditory. Others really need to have slides or a video presentation in order to understand, visual. And still others learn best when they can actually do something, like attend a lab. Each of us concentrates most easily and is most attentive when using our preferred sensory channel. No one consciously decides his decision strategy. Our preferences are established very early in life, most likely within the first six months.

The question for decision strategy.
The following question reveals your decision strategy. Please answer it for yourself. How do you know that your supplier, accountant, lawyer, a coworker is good at their job?

How to interpret what you hear.
Our language is full of cues to our decision strategy, but you will hear it most clearly in the verbs people select when answering this question.

Visual. A visual person will answer the decision strategy question like this. "I see them do their work, through observation. I watch what they do and look at the results. They have to show me they without what they're doing." Visual people talk about the world and their experience in visual words and phrases. They focus and view and observe. Asked to recall a mountain scene, they'll describe the deep green forest, dappled in light, the crystal clear water reflecting a cloudless blue sky. They live in a world of sight relationships. The look for information.

Auditory. Auditory people answer the question with sound verbs. "I ask questions and they tell me what they know. We talk. I hear how they are doing from the people they work with. I know he's good at his job because he puts it in layman's terms when he explains it to you." An auditory person listens, keeps his or her ears open, and asks questions that others respond to verbally. From the mountain scene, they will remark on the sound of the water, the bird songs, and the wind in the trees. When they talk about their experience, which auditory people will do quite readily, they will use verbs like those. They live in a world of sound relationships. They listen for information.

Feelings. Feelings people answer the coworker question like this. "I have to work with them. We must develop it together. I know he's good at hi job because he does it the way it do. The language of a feelings person is full of references to doing thing. They work with and follow and do. They will recall the temperature of the day and the water at the mountain stream, how heavy the rocks were, and whether they slippery. They live in a world of spatial and tactile relationships.

How decision strategy affects the sales cycle.
Many communications problems arise because of mismatched decision strategies. For example, when an auditory salesperson tells a visual prospect the benefits of the product or tries to close that person over the phone, he or she creates a barrier instead of a bridge. Because the salesperson is convinced by hearing things, he or she unconsciously assumes that everyone is convinced the same way. When a customer's attention starts to wane, this person typically responds by increasing the word

52

count or volume, or both. Of course, that causes the visual process to glaze over even more. What is needed in that situation is less tell and more show, visual aids, photographs, brochures, charts, or pretty pictures and minimal phone contact.

A friend recently told us how she observed decision strategies working out in her office. Her boss, Allen, bought a new computer program for the telemarketing division. The salesperson showed him all sorts of information, including an impressively illustrated operating manual. A classic visual, Allen bought the package, but not the optional classroom training. He felt confident his team could learn the program from the book. It looked straightforward, and there were lots of pictures. Unfortunately, his staff was primarily auditory, as telemarketers naturally tend to be, and had difficultly learning from books. They needed to hear how the program worked. They needed to ask questions and listen to instructions, and put in a variety of terms. They needed things worded and reworded. From their standpoint, the best the book could do was supplement verbal training.

After a week of struggling with the incredibly clear and simple, Allen's words, instruction manual, the telemarketing division was essentially at a standstill. Desperate and mystified, visual Allen agreed to purchase the optional training. Within half a day, everyone in the office was fluent in the program.

As a salesperson, your job is to convince people that your product or service is the best one available. Matching their decision strategy is the first step in that process. When you can deliver your information to your customers on their most active sensory channel, you will begin to sell the way they buy. Delivering your message through unused channels results in frustration and failure.

Using decision strategies to presell your client.
Now that you know the distinctions among the three decision
strategies, you will easily spot them in conversation. Your
evaluation of your client's sensory preference should cover your
whole presentation. Do not make the common mistake of
giving information the way you like to receive it. Adapt your
language and your presentation to your audience, and fatter
commission checks will be your reward.

Preselling the visual customer.
Part of gaining rapport with a visual person involves using
visual language. Do not say, "I understand what you're saying."
Instead, agree by saying, "I see what you mean." On the phone,
make word pictures. When you visit them, take plenty of visual
props, and show them liberally. These customers will absorb
that visual information more effectively than any words you
speak. Don't be offended if they pay more attention to your
props than to you. As you talk to them, invite them to look
things over and see for themselves. If you're visual, you will
naturally use these phrases. But if you're not, you will increase
your ability to communicate with visual people by getting
familiar with the list of the visual verbs.

Preselling the auditory customer.
Gaining rapport with auditory people begins by using their
sensory verbs. Say things like, "I hear what you're saying,"
instead of, "I see what you mean." Rather than, "Let's get
together. Let's talk Friday. Let me talk about, not, "Let me
show you our newest."

When making a sales call to an auditory it isn't necessary to
bring along your visual aids,. For the most part, they will not
look at them unless you explain them. Even then, they are
unlikely to recall them or give them much weight in their final
decision. At most times, they are comfortable with phone

contact, and they often like to talk. If you are visual, you will want to familiarize yourself with the auditory verbs.

Preselling the feelings customer.
Calling on a feelings client requires you to match their hands-on style of learning. This can often be challenging to visual and auditory people. Be sure to have props that they can touch and hold, even if it's nothing more than a giveaway pen. Fiddling with things helps them take in and sort information. They won't necessarily seem to be listening at time, but they will be taking it in. When talking to a feelings prospect, focus on action verbs and the activities involved in what you're doing. They are very especially aware. So be liberal with dimensions and locations. Our offices are at the corner of Ledbetter and Hawthorn. Come and visit us once we've gone through the plan together, you'll know how we do things. Emphasize how much you want to work with them, to track down the problem and develop solutions, and do it just the way you would do it.

It probably seems like we are overemphasizing something as seemingly as trivial as the verse you use in a sentence, but we're not. Rapport is a very subtle and unconscious experience. The accumulation of these trivial events is what creates affinity between people. If you look at things the way I look at things or hear them the way I hear them or do them the way I do them, I can trust you more than those who see or hear or do those same things differently.

When you match a person's sensory preference they intuit your alignment with their perception of the world, just as when you match their criteria words, they instinctively believe you understand what they want. The more conscious you can become of the unconscious components that make up rapport, the more likely you will create it consciously in your relationships. To convince yourself how easy and accurate this is, we suggest that you spend several days just asking this one question. How do you know that someone is good at their job?

You will quickly develop the ability to hear and evaluate the clues to decision strategy.

Once you know a persons style, use the appropriate language in your conversation. Then intentionally them and observe, listen, or feel any changes in the quality of the interaction. Within a very short time, you will be able to discern decision strategy in normal speech and will no longer need to ask the questions.

Alternative questions.
You may not always be able to ask the question exactly as posed at the beginning of this chapter. You can ask the question in several ways, but the object of the question must always be another person, never the prospect.

If you ask the customer how he knows he's good at his own job. You'll earn his motivating source, not his decision strategy. Also you must word the question in such a way they have tell you about a specific person, and not refer to abstract qualities. Following are examples that may fit more easily into the selling environment. The emphasized words are the significant ones.

How did you know your last supplier did a good job? How did you know they did a good job? How do you know that your employees are doing a good job? What is your decision strategy? How did you answer the question, "How do you know that your supplier, accountant, lawyer, coworker, is good at their job?" Are you visual, auditory, or feelings? The odds are, that you're visual. *There are millions of people in the other two categories and many more who combine two.*

Practice makes perfect. The patterns for decisions strategy quickly become clear as you tune your own perception to hearing them in other people's speech. What verbs and figures of speech do they put into their conversation? Do they see, hear , or feel?

Example 1: <u>Paul</u>, "Anne, you've worked with a consultant before in your company. I was wondering how you knew that they were doing a good job." <u>Anne</u>, "That was easy. All I had to do was listen to the feedback from the production department."

Example 2: <u>Bruce,</u> "Earlier you mentioned that you had worked a consultant before and had been satisfied with their work. I was wondering how you knew that they had done a good job." <u>Paula,</u> "They were always in on time. And when I talked to them they could explain to me in detail what they were doing. I just got the feeling that they knew their stuff."

Example 3: <u>Carol,</u> "Based on your press relationship, how did you know that Sue was really intent on making it work?" <u>Brett,</u> "When we get together, we just seem to blend into each other's thoughts."

Example 4: <u>Linda,</u> "How do you know that you've got a good relationship?" <u>Janice,</u> "I really notice how he talks to me and the things he does for me. I get lots of cards for no special reason, and I can read the depth of his feeling in the messages. This boy is for real." Reviewing further is essential to learning how to distinguish the patterns in decisions strategy. We suggest you ask this question in a variety of contexts of anyone who let you record their answer. At home, play their answers until you're sure whether they're visual, auditory, or feelings.

Chapter 7
Is it Really What You say that Convinces Your Customer

You know that making a sale is nothing more than convincing your customer that you have what they need. What complicates this simple truth is this reality. Every person becomes convinced in a different way. Each of us has a strategy by which we make decisions within a given context, whether it's choosing a car, or choosing a stall in a public restroom. The convincer strategy is the means by which we decide, because it lets us know whether or not our criteria are met. When you move a customer to decision, you have met the requirements of his or her convincer strategy. We each have our method, and though it is unconscious, we know exactly what it is and whether or not it has been met. Knowing how your prospects are convinced will save untold anxiety. This knowledge will keep you from bothering them for an answer, because you will know when they're ready to decide.

Convincer strategies. This part of the human operating system comprises four patterns, automatic, consistent, number of examples, and time period. These four patterns are simple to distinguish from one another, and easy to recognize as you will discover.

Automatic. Most people would characterize an automatic as someone who jumps right in. This person does not need to have seen, heard, or done a thing to believe that he or she can do it. This person has a high trust level. As an example, an automatic shopper never compares prices or checks out other brands. If he or she wants a radio, for instance, the first radio seen will suit just fine. Essentially, automatics need no proof, because they are automatically convinced.

Consistent.
The consistent pattern is exactly opposite the automatic. This person has a low level of trust. A consistent evaluates constantly. Just because Café Nuar was good last week, does not mean it will be good tonight. This person is essentially never convinced. Every day is a new day. Consistent pattern typically holds no preconceived notions, and require regular re-convincing. As a client, they can be frustrating because they will not cut you much slack or let you rest on your laurels. In the shopping example, a consistent would need to check out several sources before buying a radio, and even then, may not be convinced until he or she uses the product for some time.

Number of examples.
A number of examples person needs to see, hear, or do something a number of times to be convinced. The number varies from person to person, of course. However, an examples person will always answer the question with a specific number. It may be one. It may be two. It may be 20. However, it is the magic number. Attempting to make them decide before they have had the requisite number of examples will only irritate them and frustrate you. A three-example person buying cat foods, either needs to evaluate different samples, brands, sizes, or flavors before deciding.

Time period.
People with the time period pattern require a time interval before they decide. They are specific about that interval. It may be two hours, two days, two weeks, or longer. No matter how short or long the intervals, time period people must have that amount of time or they will not convinced.

The question for convincer strategy.
The question for convincer strategy relates to the previous one. How do you know that someone is good at their job? How many times do they have to demonstrate that they are good at their job, before you are convinced?

59

How to interpret what you hear.
This is among the easiest patterns to distinguish in response to
the question. Even though their convincer strategy is in the
deep background of human operating system, people's answers
slide off their tongues as if they had been waiting for this one
question all their lives.

An **automatic** will respond with answers like these, "I give
people the benefit of the doubt. I assume they are good at their
job or they would not be in it. I just have to see them do it and I
know whether they can. I just trust that people can do the job."

Consistent individuals respond in this way. "I never believe
someone's good at their job. They have to show me every day.
Just because they can do it today, does not mean they can do it
tomorrow. Things change. You can't count on people to be
consistent."

Number of Examples people always answer with a number. "I
have to see him do it four times. Then I know. If you hear from
five different people that they know what they are doing, you
can be sure they do. After I've done it with them twice, I can
tell."

Time Period people respond as if the question were, "How long
do they have to demonstrate?" They respond like this. "It takes
me a couple of days of working with them to know for sure. If
I can watch them for two hours. I will always know. If don't
hear any complaints for week, they know what they're doing."

Convincer strategies are crucial to decision-making. Decision
Strategy and Convincer Strategy together give you vital input
about how a person takes in information and how he or she
processes it to decide. Knowing this, gives you a big advantage
because it allows you to give your customer information in a
way and in proportions that remove obstacles to making

60

decisions. Let us take as an illustration, a person who is visual and number of times. It is not necessarily to make five separate sales calls to persuade the client to buy from you. After your initial call, you can send four different mailings relating to your product, or you may break one sales call into five examples by taking along visual props that you can bring out one at a time. That can add up to the magic five count.

As another example, let us take prospects that are auditory, time, two weeks. Once you have made the initial call, you can wait patiently, or you can make a couple of courtesy calls in the interim to ensure that you stay on the list. Whatever you do, do not contact this person with the expectation of an order then. Just be patient for two weeks and you will do your case a lot more good. If you are not the patient type, however, you can speed up the process. See the example below:

Marvin once had to sell to a man whose convincer strategy was six months. You can be sure many sales representatives gave up in frustration long before they got an answer. Marvin did not want to wait that long, however, so he arranged for his BOS program to think that amount of time passed. During the sales call, he asked him to recall what he was doing six months before. The man named off several things. At that point, Marvin made the sale presentation again. The client laughed, saying he had already seen it. Marvin put the presentation away and started bringing him forward in time by talking about things that had happened in the interim until they were once again in the present. Then he showed the presentation again saying, "I showed you this presentation six months ago. What do you think about it?" He laughed because they both knew it was a game, but his BOS program did not. It associated the presentation with six months previous, and he bought the program that day.

In the case of a consistent client, being forewarned is being forearmed. Be prepared to prove yourself and your wares every time you go in. Be consistent in everything you do with them. Be on time. Follow through on what you say you will do when you say you will it. Do not substitute things you have promised. In other words, be ready to be put through your paces. They are unlikely ever to cut you any slack. One mistake and you can be history.

For a consistent, inconsistency is practically intolerable. One chink in this armor is that a consistent has never bought anything he or she was completely convinced was perfect. You can play to that by recalling some earlier buying experience. Remember when you bought your color television set and then say something like, "This is just like that." You will not be convinced until you buy it and try it out.

The key to selling to automatics is creating rapport and building trust. A crucial step in that process is matching their decision strategy in your language. Use the other means of creating rapport that we have outlined, and an automatic will trust you. If you match all their BOS components and they need your product, they will buy from you. One problem does occur occasionally in selling to automatics. If you or your product in any way resembles or reminds them of someone or something that they do not trust, they will automatically associate you with that person or product.

After you have practiced identifying decision strategies, add the convincer strategy question to get the full range of information about how a person learns, is convinced, and decides. Once you have them pegged, think of creative ways to match their convincer strategy and move them to a decision. Practice on everyone. Attempt to convince them to go to your favorite restaurant or to a particular movie. Challenge yourself to give them what they need in order to make the decision you want them to make.

Alternative question.

How many times do others have to be successful before you are convinced they know what they are doing? What is your convincer strategy? How did you answer the question? Are you automatic, consistent, examples, or time period? Understand your BOS profile so you can prevent yourself from assuming that everyone thinks alike. Knowing your own BOS profile gives you the freedom to match the person you are addressing. At this point, we would like to complete the story from the previous chapter regarding the printing company owner and the inspector from Washington DC.

You may recall that while the inspector was purchasing the belt for his son, he looked at three belts, indicating to the printer, who was a keen observer of BOS cues, that the inspector was visual, and three examples. When they returned to the plant, the owner showed the inspector the printing results three separate times, while pointing out how the quality matched the specific criteria within their request for proposal. The sale was completed before the inspector left town, and the contract was initiated.

People know what convinces them, and they remain unconvinced until that criterion is met. Knowing a person's convincer strategy will save you untold aggravation in giving your clients information in exactly the manner that convinces them.

Practice makes perfect. The patterns for convincer strategy are simple to decipher. Does the person answer with a number or a time period? Do they trust easily, or do they withhold trust in lieu of a consistent performance?

Example 1: Madison, "Working with a lawyer on critical cases, you have to have a trusting relationship. How many times did he have to do a good job before you were convinced that he was a good attorney?" <u>Roger</u>, "You're right. When you are in court, your future depends on that person and whether he can support you professionally. How long? Let me see. Probably the third time he presented a case, I could tell. After that, I knew he could do a good job for us.

Example 2: <u>Lynn,</u> "I've had such a hard time finding a doctor, and you seem so pleased with yours. How many times did she have to demonstrate that she was good doctor before you were convinced?" <u>Shirley</u>, "My doctor? She has to prove it every time. Things change too fast in that profession and so do I. My condition is different every day. She just doesn't get to rest on her laurels. I just can't treat my health like that."

Example 3: <u>Mark</u>, "You've worked with brokers before and had some good relationships. How often would he have to do a good job for you before you really trusted him?" <u>Judy</u>, "I've worked with three brokers over the last five years. And I knew they were good when I gave them my money to invest. I wouldn't have worked with them if I hadn't thought they knew their business."

Example 4: <u>Leroy</u>, "I've got a pile of dirty shirts up to my knees because I just can't find a cleaner that I can trust. I'm beginning to think that I'm unreasonable. Tell me, Tara, how many times do you think somebody has to do a good job before you're convinced?" <u>Tara</u>, "It just takes time, Leroy. I figure about four months. If they haven't done anything wrong, then they probably know what they're doing and you don't have to worry anymore."

Reviewing further is essential in learning how to distinguish the convincer strategy patterns. We suggest you ask this question in a variety of contexts of anyone who will let you record their answer. At home, play their answers until you are sure whether they are giving a timeframe, a number of examples, are automatically convinced, or are never convinced.

Answers to the review.
Example 1: <u>Roger,</u> "You're right. When you are in court, your future depends on that person and whether he can support you professionally. How long? Let me see. Probably the third time he presented a case, I could tell. After that, I knew he could do a good job for us." Roger is three examples.

Example 2: <u>Shirley,</u> "My doctor? She has to prove it every time. Things change too fast in that profession and so do I. My condition is different every day. She just doesn't get to rest on her laurels. I just can't treat my health like that." Shirley is consistent.

Example 3: <u>Judy,</u> "I've worked with three brokers over the last five years. And I knew they were good when I gave them my money to invest. I wouldn't have worked with them if I hadn't thought they knew their business." Judy is automatic. She knows going in and doesn't need to be convinced.

Example 4: <u>Tara,</u> "It just takes time, Leroy. I figure about four months. If they haven't done anything wrong, then they probably know what they're doing and you don't have to worry anymore." Tara is time, four months.

Here is a quick review of Chapters 5-7:

Jacob the consultant calls Miller, his potential customers. Can you decipher his BOS profile for **process approach, decision strategy, and convincer strategy?**
<u>Jacob</u> "Good afternoon, Mr. Miller, I'm calling you as requested to confirm a time to meet with your accounts receivable manager. Is he okay for the middle of the week?"
<u>Miller,</u> "Yes, Thursday morning will be fine for him, and I'll be available on and off during the day to meet with you." <u>Jacob</u> "By the way, Mr. Miller, I forgot to ask you a question while I was there. *"I'm curious why you chose the consultants you*

used last time."

Miller, "Well, Mr. Jacob I think I mentioned that before that they were good at what they did and they answered all my questions satisfactorily. They also had great references." Jacob, "Great. That answers my question. Shall I ask for you when I arrive on Thursday morning?" Miller, "Yes. You can be here at 7:30 a.m. so we and talk a little more before I set you up with the manager." Jacob "Sure I'll be there at 7:30 a.m. Do you want me to bring some donuts?" Miller, "I'll tell you what. Mix and match some pastries and I'll supply the coffee." Jacob "Sounds great. I will make sure we have plenty of choices. I'll be there Thursday."

Thursday morning arrives. Jacob "Good morning, Mr. Miller. I was tempted to eat these pastries, but I thought I'd better give you first choice." Miller, "I appreciate that. Let's have coffee in my office. There are a few things I want you to know before you meet the manager." Jacob "Mr. Miller, when you used the other consulting firm, how did you know they were doing a good job when they were in your operation?" Miller, "Well, that was pretty easy to tell. The meetings we had after each day told me that they understood my business and could get to the heart of the problems. Also, the employees gave me good feedback. The end result, of course, was a system that works. I didn't hear one complaint about the new process after they left."

Jacob, "Great. Well, what do you want to tell me before we meet the manager?" Miller, "This is strictly confidential. I would like you to evaluate whether you think the manager is capable of handling accounts receivable at the level it's growing. Can you give me some feedback on that before you leave today?" Jacob, "I'll be glad to tell you what I think." Miller, "Thanks. By the way, why didn't you get some pastries with apple filling? Those are my favorite." Jacob, "I'll remember that the next time we meet. I want to compliment you on your assistant. She's really professional and knows her business well."

66

Miller, "She's worked for me for about two years and probably could handle my job." Jacob, "I hired a research person about a month ago, and finding people you can depend on these days is getting to be a big challenge. I'm wondering, how often do you think a person has to do a good job before you're convinced they're capable?" Miller, "You may find this hard to believe, Mr. Jacob, but I can tell almost immediately. I knew my assistant would be good when I finished interviewing her." Jacob, "I guess I felt that way, too. But there are times when I question myself. I guess that keeps us on our toes." Miller, "You're right about that. Now let's go meet the manager and put you to work."

Answers to the review.
Process approach. Mr. Miller is options. He answered completely with criteria words and not procedure. He answered a why question.

Decision strategy. He is auditory. He knows because he hears it said.

Convincer strategy. He is automatic. He knows immediately.

Chapter 8
When to Talk too Much

Have you ever noticed how differently people eat? Some
people cut their food into small pieces, while others hardly use a
knife at all and gulp huge mouthfuls.

Process scope.
Were like that about how we take in information. Some people
like it in small bite-sized pieces, while others prefer big chunks.
When you know your client's process scope, it's easy to give
your sales presentation in just the chunk size the client likes.
Process scope consists of a continuum between two patterns,
general and specific.

General. The general person concentrates on the big picture
and works best when he or she can delegate the details. This
person tends to look at the world through a wide-angle lens.
These individuals are most comfortable at the concept level and
struggle to follow the step-by-step procedures required to bring
a project to completion. To them, the parts of a system are
unrelated, a random set. Details are easily overlooked when
giving directions, and easily forgotten when receiving them.

Specific. If the general use a wide-angle lens, the specific uses
a microscopic one. He or she will only see the whole picture
when it's loaded with details. Often, this person is so focused
on the immediate task that he or she does not conceive of how it
relates to a larger goal. This person defines tasks in terms of
sequences, not purposes. "I do this, then this, then that." Not,
"I do this because it's required for my taxes." If this person
doesn't develop a detailed plan for a task, or doesn't get one
from someone else, he or she will be lost and won't begin to
work. To a person who is fully specific, there has never been
too much detail.

General and specific are the end points on a continuum of behavior. A great many people are not fully one or the other. Your prospects will require varying levels of detail. It is important to match that level when making your presentation; because that is the precise amount of detail, they want from you. This category of the human operating system determines the style of language that will establish rapport between the two of you, whether it is spare or full of details.

In a selling situation, listen to the customer's response to any of your questions. If you do not have a clear moving picture of what was said, then the customer is someone who sorts information more generally. As the customer gives more detail, they sort more specifically. We recall a customer telling about a problem that he and his wife had concerning investment. Whenever the man wanted to invest in a part product or piece of real estate, he would go home and basically tell his wife, "I have a great investment opportunity for us. It's a piece of property, and the returns will be excellent. We'll be able to get out of it in a few years and make some money."

Whenever he did this, he said that his wife would look at him very oddly and say, "What are you talking about? How can we put our money in something like that? Tell me more about it. What kind of investment is it? Where is it? How much money do we have to put in? What does the market research show?" She would barrage him with specific questions until the customer said he would get pretty upset. With that kind of intense questioning, he thought his wife didn't trust his judgment. But it actually was nothing that serious. The fact was that he took in information in big chunks, and wife wanted information in lots of small pieces.

Of course, at that point, we knew that we should be more general in our presentation. However, if we were selling to his wife, we would be ready to give plenty of details.

Question for process scope. "Tell me about one of your favorite working experiences." Movies or books will also do as a context. The request must be answered with a one-time event.

How to interpret what you hear. Modifiers are the first clue in identifying these patterns. A specific fills his or her speech with adjectives and adverbs. When answering your inquiry about a favorite experience, count the modifiers. A total specific will often use two or more per sentence. This person will also give concrete examples. "I saw a great film last Tuesday, the 16th. We also go to the early show because it's only $2.50 then. They were showing a double-feature of *Cool Hand Luke* and *The Verdict*. I just love Paul Newman's blue eyes and the way he talked so soft and slow." That would be just the beginning, for a specific will happily tell you the entire cast as well as the plot of both movies.

If they tell it to you in sequence then you will have a procedure as well as a specific. Be sure to give these people plenty of time because they won't feel complete if they get to tell the whole story from beginning to end. The general person will answer the movie question simply, "I like going to movies." Getting details requires interrogation, asking specific questions and sometimes asking them more than once.

Dialogue A. <u>Julie</u>, "Gene, we talked about what you want in an automobile, and I believe I can help you. I'm wondering, could you tell me about the last favorable experience you had when buying a car?" <u>Gene</u>, "This is the first car I ever bought." <u>Julie</u>, "I see. I am curious. What was the last item you purchased that gave you the same criteria you're looking for in an automobile, quality, dependability?" <u>Gene</u>, "Well, I've been wanting an electric razor for some time, and I thought, why not? I have been cutting myself with razor blades too long. So just the other day, Tuesday, to be exact, I went shopping for an electric razor. I got up at 7:00 a.m. I did not shave, because I wanted to try each razor until I found one that did a good job, a smooth cut

70

without pain. I had breakfast close to the mall and then immediately started to shop when the stores opened at 9:00 a.m. I went to three stores before I found the right razor. It was Remington with all the bells and whistles. I shaved what was left after six trial shaves with other razors, and made the decision on the spot. You know when you've found the right thing."

Well, obviously, Gene thrives on detail. A key to deciding whether someone is specific is whether you can get a clear understanding of what they're talking about. Is it like a movie, or more like snapshots? The key is the amount of detail. Gene averages more than one per sentence in this paragraph, and that would be the level specificity if he would feel most comfortable when Julie responds. Gene also exhibits a procedures pattern because of the way he sequences the story. And he also demonstrates the speech pattern of an internal in the last line.

Dialogue B. Julie, "I'm curious, Tom. What was the last item you purchased that gave you the same criteria you're looking for in an automobile, quality, dependability?" Tom, "I'd bought an electric razor last week. It was something I'd wanted for some time." Tom only uses two modifiers, "electric," and "last," which in this context are hardly enlightening details. His sequence is reversed. He tells us his behavior, and then what motivated it.

The answers you get from clients may not be so pronounced; however, they will be filled with clues. In evaluating their answers, listen for modifiers and sequences. Specific dates or times indicate both detail and sequence, strong evidence of a specific speech pattern. Abstract examples and generalities turn up in the typically brief answers of a general pattern. They will ignore your request for a specific event, and answer with a vague range of behaviors. "I like going to movies. I liked working in the benefits department. I really enjoy fishing in the summer." They tend to summarize where a specific will elaborate.

How process scope affects the sales cycle. As with the other patterns, the key to using process scope is matching your prospect's language pattern in your own speech, which creates rapport. A person who feels comfortable with the big picture will feel frustrated ad oppressed by too many particulars. When presenting your information to a general, concentrate on the overall direction and don't spend a lot of time on the smaller details. If you do, they will quickly get bored, trance out, and pay no attention to your presentation.

Here is how you might deal with a general. "Tom, as you drive this car, you may notice the overall ride and the feel of solid construction along with smoothness. Having a car that's stylish and dependable, along with the other benefits is something that you said you wanted, isn't it?" When selling to a specific, put your information into small chunks and concentrate on the details.

Specifics do not concern themselves with the outcome so much as with the steps involved. Rather than give them a short summary of what your product will do, break it down into a series of how it will benefit them. They feel cheated by generalities. If you fail to give them information in the small chunks with which they're comfortable, they will be frustrated and seek out other sources. In order to decide, they need specifics. Otherwise, they will refuse to decide, on grounds of insufficient data. It is your job to see that they have that information.

"Tom, as you drive this car, you may notice how solid it feels because of the extra suspension and oversized motor mounts that are standard on this car only. And with that added advantage, you might notice how smooth it feels. The tires are a new design with a split wedge for greater safety on slick surfaces, and more cushion on bumpy roads. The details of this car, like the rolled in the seats that give them extra strength, add to the style. Notice the advanced gauges, like a Boeing 707, and how easy they are to read as you're driving at night, they really add to your ability to see without distracting you from the road."

If you cannot find a way to work this question in your initial inquiries with the customer, you can still identify the pattern by listening closely to their answers to the other questions. A general, will always answer in generalities, and with abstract examples. Specifics will respond in detailed sequenced and concrete examples. The more detail your customer gives you, the more he or she will want from you. When you match that level of detail, they will feel synchronized with you.

For a few days, practice only this question with your friends and colleagues. It will not take you long to feel comfortable identifying this speech pattern in others. Once you know what pattern they are, match them in their level of detail, and watch how they respond. There are many things, body language, voice tone and inflection, willingness to answer, that will tell you whether you're in rapport with someone. Once you have rapport, deliberately mismatch them, and observe the response. You will quickly discover the powerful effects of process scope in creating effective communication.

What is your process scope? How did you answer the question? Did you tell a story in a sequence? Would someone reading or hearing your answer know the details of your experience, or would they be lost, knowing only the overall direction? How big were the chunks of information you answered with? Did you give abstract examples or concrete ones?

Practice makes perfect. The patterns for process scope are simple to decipher. Does the person answer with a story full of details, or do they leave you with just the barest understanding of their situation?

Example 1: Susan, "Bill, I know you've bought equipment like this before, and I'm very happy you're interested in our equipment. Could you tell me about your experience with your other vendor?" Bill, "When we started out with our first big order about seven years ago, I would have never guessed that someday I'd be big enough to go directly to the manufacturer. But we've grown so fast. We've increased our sales by more than 12 percent each of the last five years. In that time, we've doubled our sales force, and the distributors, like Henry's company – Henry was our old rep – just could not give us the kind of delivery we needed. We've refined our procedures around here until we pretty much run on next-day delivery. Plus, the shipping costs were mounting because their distribution center was near Denver. Shipping had gone from 1 to 3 percent of cost, and we just couldn't see how it was ever going to come down. It was just a matter of getting too big, I guess."

Example 2: Tori, "Heather, would you tell me about the last movie you saw that you liked?" Heather, "Oh, I loved that movie with Laura what's her name. You know the one. It was romantic comedy. It was out last year sometime. They were so cute together, but I'd never seen him in anything. It was just one of those real sweet movies."

Example 3: John, "Carmen, you sound excited about going on vacation. Could you tell me about the last time you had fun on a vacation?" Carmen, Now that would be easy. Bob and I took a Caribbean cruise three years ago and it was to die for. We made seven ports of call in eight days. No phones, fabulous food, just everything you could possibly want. More food than an Army could eat. Brenda Banks, the famous singer, did two shows. Bob drove golf balls off the bough. I got a massage every day. We had the most romantic night in St. Martin. And then Bob lost $150.00 at the casino in San Juan. Everything was just perfect, and it didn't cost but about $760.00 each, plus the airfare. It was a bargain.

74

Example 4: <u>Mason</u>, "We've been trying for an hour to decide where we're going to go eat. Why don't you tell me about your favorite eating experience and that will help me think up some alternatives." <u>Sylvia</u>, "Let's see. The one that really sticks out goes back a long way. I was dating a guy who later became my first husband. I think it was probably our first date and he took me to this place on the harbor. It was like a dive, I thought. But inside, it was really charming. Mediterranean, candles in potbellied rafino bottles, that kinda thing. All seafood menus, incredible selection. I'd never had crab, and we shared Alaska king crab legs. And he was being so sweet. I fell in love that night. We used to go there for anniversaries."

Reviewing further is essential to learning how to distinguish the patterns in process scope. We suggest you ask this question in a variety of contexts of anyone who let you record their answer on tape. At home, play their answers. It will take very few examples for you to begin to see the various levels of detail people use. Some pour it on; others sprinkle it. And still others dole out specifics as if they were gold nuggets.

Answers to the review.
Example 1: <u>Bill,</u> "When we started out with our first big order about seven years ago, I would have never guessed that someday I'd be big enough to go directly to the manufacturer. But we've grown so fast. We've increased our sales by more than 12 percent each of the last five years. In that time, we've doubled our sales force, and the distributors, like Henry's company – Henry was our old rep – just couldn't give us the kind of delivery we needed. We've refined our procedures around here until we pretty much run on next-day delivery. Plus, the shipping costs were mounting because their distribution center was near Denver. Shipping had gone from 1 to 3 percent of cost, and we just couldn't see how it was ever going to come down. It was just a matter of getting too big, I guess."

Bill is a specific. He feels comfortable with a high level of numbers and facts. One specific per sentence would suit him just fine.

Example 2: Heather, "Oh, I loved that movie with Laura what's her name. You know the one. It was romantic comedy. It was out last year sometime. They were so cute together, but I'd never seen him in anything. It was just one of those real sweet movies." Heather is a general. She edits out details and feels comfortable with an overall picture.

Example 3: Carmen, "Now that would be easy. Bob and I took a Caribbean cruise three years ago and it was to die for. We made seven ports of call in eight days. No phones, fabulous food, just everything you could possibly want. More food than an Army could eat. Brenda Banks, the famous singer, did two shows. Bob drove golf balls off the bough. I got a massage every day. We had the most romantic night in St. Martin. And then Bob lost $150.00 at the casino in San Juan. Everything was just perfect, and it didn't cost but about $760.00 each, plus the airfare. It was a bargain." Carmen is definitely a specific.

Example 4: Sylvia, "Let's see. The one that really sticks out goes back a long way. I was dating a guy who later became my first husband. I think it was probably our first date and he took me to this place on the harbor. It was like a dive, I thought. However, inside, it was charming. Mediterranean, candles in pot bellied rafino bottles, that kinda thing. All seafood menus, incredible selection. I'd never had crab, and we shared Alaska king crab legs. In addition, he was being so sweet. I fell in love that night. We used to go there for anniversaries." Sylvia is more general than specific. She does throw in a few details, about one every other sentence, but she does not crave them. She will be most comfortable with a moderate level of detail.

Chapter 9
Client Disagreement Can Close the Sale

When you look at individual examples of things, do you compare them, that is note how they are the same, or do you contrast them, by which we mean concentrate on how they are different. Comparing and contrasting. That is how we learn. There is no other way short of divine revelation. Whether you distinguish through similarities or differences defines your process relationship.

Process relationship

Four patterns make up this category, same, same differences, difference, and different same. These patterns are potent factors for rapport building and information transfer. Think of them as processing strategies. It is crucial that you know a person's processing strategy if you want to influence this person, such as getting him or her to understand how good your product is. When you match their strategy, you have the edge in getting them to understand what you tell them.

Same: The same individual likes the world to stay calm and regular. This person thrives on routine and does not seek new challenges or experiment with new approaches to work. In fact, if too much change is introduced at the meeting, for instance, he or she will likely build stress and break rapport. Same people typically stay with one product or service for long periods of time, as long as the sameness matches their criteria. They strive for normalcy. These people are often considered inflexible because they simply will not broach change. Any change distresses them and they adapt to it poorly.

Same difference: A person with this pattern appreciates regularity and normalcy, and at the same time, requires variety. If work does not provide it, this person will initiate it, seeking out new but related activities. He or she enjoys finding new ways of doing things and improving on routines, adapts well to change, and will follow through on long-term projects. When speaking with a same difference person, it's important to balance sameness with a new approach.

Difference and difference same: People with these patterns thrive on change. In fact, to be happy, they must have new and different activities or leading-edge products, or new and different approaches to service. They do not tolerate routines, and will force change in order to satisfy this pattern. If they cannot make that happen, they will change suppliers. They are sometimes experienced as people who disagree a lot with the opinions of other people.

The question for process relationship:
The following question elicits responses that reveal a person's process relationship. What is the relationship between what you were doing this year on your job and what you did last year on your job?

How to interpret what you hear:
Same and difference patterns answer the relationship question with opposite responses. You only need listen for whether you how things are the same or how they are different.

Dialogue A. <u>Sue,</u> "Bill, we haven't had an opportunity to talk about your business. And I know that when I learn more about how you developed and grew your company, I'll be able to see how my services will be more useful to you. I'm curious about the relationship between what your business was like last year and what you are doing this year." <u>Bill,</u> "I don't know how that can help you, but I can tell you that it's totally different. If you stay on the same track, you fall into a rut. This year, we're focusing on the international market almost exclusively. Last year, we concentrated on building our domestic network."

Dialogue B. <u>Sue,</u> "Bob, we haven't had an opportunity to talk about your business. And I know that when I learn more about how you developed and grew your company, I'll be able to see how my services will be more useful to you. I'm curious about the relationship between what your business was like last year and what you are doing this year." <u>Bob</u>, "Sue, that's a good question. When I really think about it, I believe that the business is basically the same. We don't change things when they're working."

Dialogue C. <u>Sue</u>, "Barney, we haven't had an opportunity to talk about your business. And I know that when I learn more about how you developed and grew your company, I'll be able to see how my services will be more useful to you. I'm curious about the relationship between what your business was like last year and what you are doing this year." <u>Barney,</u> "I'd have to say it's pretty much the same, only better. You're hopefully always improving. It's the same business, the same customers, and deadlines, but we seem to handle them with more grace, and definitely finesse better at what we don't know.

Dialogue D. <u>Sue</u>. "Bailey, we haven't had an opportunity to talk about your business. And I know that when I learn more about how you developed and grew your company, I'll be able to see how my services will be more useful to you. I'm curious about the relationship between what your business was like last year and what you are doing this year." <u>Bailey</u>, "When I think about all the changes, well, it's almost not the same business, new personnel, new machines, new customers, but the same products and the same suppliers. Therefore, it all balances out.

People almost always answer the relationship question with patterns this clear. You can easily see that Bill in Dialogue A is the difference pattern. By questioning what good that does her, he even differences the reason for that question. Then he tells Sue that his business is totally different. They aren't even dealing with the same market. But you're probably asking

79

yourself, "What if the business really has changed? How else could Bill answer then?" The actual state or rate of change doesn't matter in identifying the pattern because if Bill were a same, he would have found something that was the same to answer with. "We're making the same product. We're still at the same address. We have the same employees." There would be many things that hadn't changed, and a same person would focus on those.

On the other hand, a difference person will find how things are different because that is what relationship means to them. In Dialogue B, Bob is a same. He sees how this year is the same as last year, and makes no distinction between the two. Were there really no differences worth mentioning? Unlikely, but Bob does not concentrate on that. Sue asked for the relationship and that is what relationship means to him, how things are the same.

In Dialogue C, Bailey tells Sue how things are the same, and then adds how they are different. Whenever you hear comparative words like "more, better," and, "improve," that is the speech pattern of same difference. They see things in terms of evolution and will emphasize gradual improvement rather than radical changes. They learn by comparing things first and then contrasting them.

In **Dialogue D**, Bailey tells Sue how this year is different, but then adds how it's the same. So he is a difference same. This speech pattern contrasts first and then compares. Whenever you hear words like, "although, but," and, "except," you are dealing with one of the split patterns. Another very strong clue or identifying any one of the patterns is how long a person has been in his or her job. If they've been there more than two years, it's unlikely that they're either of the difference patterns. If they've been in the same job, not just with the same company, more than ten years, it's likely they are a same. However, before assuming their pattern from that evidence, ask their relationship question just to make sure. You never know about

80

companies. Many internal changes can occur. They could have worked at the same place then years, and had 30 different projects, or they could have changed jobs often because their responsibilities kept changing, and that made them unhappy.

If you feel as if you're not getting a clear answer to your question, follow up their answer by asking, "The relationship then is?" and let them fill in the blank. People will almost always say, "The same, different," or use some comparative phrase with "better, less," or, "more,"

How process relationship affects the sales cycle:
Your prospect's process relationship is a crucial component of their information gathering process. Knowing that process allows you to fit your information into it, which dramatically increases the likelihood that they will be able to take in what you have to say. For example, a person who learns by calibrating how things are different, will not respond to explanations of how your product is like something else he or she is already using. For this person, it is vital that you distinguish yourself immediately if you want to make an impact. Observe the deliberating differencing in this response.

"Bill, our services provide our customers a way to expand and profit in these tough economic times because of the new techniques we use. I'm not sure these are services you can use at this time in your business growth. A company has to be positioned just right for the change." On the other hand, emphasizing difference with a same, assure communication failure and a missed sale. If you want these potential customers to grasp your presentation, explain how your product is the same as what they are using, and then distinguish yourself by saying their criteria.

Here is an example of how to touch them

"Our services have proven to be the same so our customer maintains their business in these tough economic times. Our time-proven techniques continue to support customers such as you because they are tried and tested over time and similar to other successful approaches." Our experience has shown that the majority of decision-makers you deal with are same difference people. Communicating effectively with them is simply a matter of saying their learning strategy. Explain how you are the same as what they're using, only better. They feel comfortable with comparative words like, "more, better, best," and, "improved."

In the **difference same pattern,** you treat them essentially the same as a difference, emphasizing the differences. This is the rarest strategy of the four. Both types of difference individuals are moved by phrases like, "different, changed, unique, new, "and, "revolutionary." This pattern may also be called a "mismatching" pattern as illustrated below.

During one of Marvin's training programs, a participant named Bill stated that what Marvin was saying was totally ridiculous. Bill argued that he had been in the selling business for over 25 years and really knew how to sell. This interruption was made during a presentation on how to build rapport. Marvin knew that the man did not have anything personal against him as the trainer. His brain was only sorting for differences. As Marvin approached this fellow, he aligned with him by repeating his statement that Bill knew how to sell because he had been at it for 25 years, and then said, "You may not believe this, Bill, but this information could be useful for some of these people with less experience."

With that, Marvin turned and restarted his program. However, in a few moments, Bill interrupted again by saying quite loudly, "Wait a minute. Hold it. Just wait one minute." Marvin expected some more conversation regarding mismatching, but this time Bill said, "That's exactly what I do. What you are saying is exactly what I do. I was just thinking back on the sales call I made, and I do that unconsciously." Miracle of miracles, Marvin uses a difference pattern to match him. This is how Marvin did it. Initially, he mismatched his statement to Bill by saying, "Bill, you won't believe this." Of course, Bill's brain mismatched that that is inside himself, he said, "I will believe this." That simple prologue released his ability to evaluate and analyze what Marvin was saying so he could see how it really did fit into the process of the building relationships.

Put even more simply, he mismatched, not believing, and believing. People with difference patterns will really test you until you realize how they process relationships. Before you get upset with them just realize that aggravating, as it may be they learn by contrasting things.

Alternative questions.
What is the relationship between the investment you made last year and the ones you're making this year? What is the relationship before your business activity last year and your approach to business this year?

Always ask for the relationship, not for the difference.

What is your process relationship? Evaluate your own answer to this question. Decide which pattern best identifies your learning strategy. Did you cite how things are the same or did you emphasize how they are different? Perhaps they were better.

Practice makes perfect. The question you must answer to identify process relationship is this, does the person compare or contrast? Do they look for differences and or similarities?

Example 1: <u>Kevin</u>, "Using a firm such as ours can be very rewarding when introducing a new manufacturing process.

We've discussed the way we operate, and the development of marketing campaigns over the phone. It would help me if I knew more about the relationship between the products you're selling this year and those you sold last year." Jennifer, "This year, we're selling more color and updated design. It's much more contemporary."

Example 2: Brian, "Could you explain to me the relationship between what you're marking this year and the last year's product line? Catherine, "Basically it's the same product. A winner is a winner." It is important that people have learned to trust us long-term. That's more valuable than a $1 million a year in advertising."

Example 3: Jason, "What is the relationship between what you're doing this year on your job and what you did last year?" Carl, "I guess the biggest difference is the technology and the numbers, too. But overall, it's the same business, same customers. The paperwork is different, computerized. But we're still trying to accomplish the same things day to day, keep the overhead monster at bay."

Example 4: Ronald, "Your Company has been so successful over the years. It is amazing. It just makes me wonder, what is the relationship between what you're doing this year and what you were doing last year?" Louise, "It seems to me that it changes pretty dramatically from year to year. There's so much turnover in employees and suppliers and new accounts, but it can't be all that different because, I mean, we're still selling the same products or the same kind anyway, to the same kinds of businesses."

Reviewing further is essential to learning how to distinguish the patterns in process relationship. We suggest you ask this question in a variety of contexts of anyone who will let you record their answer. At home, play their responses. You will quickly be able to distinguish whether someone is same or different, whether they compare or contrast.

Answers to the review. Example 1: <u>Jennifer</u>, "This year, we're selling more color and updated design. It's much more contemporary." Jennifer is difference. More reflects comparison.

Example 2: <u>Catherine</u>, "Basically it's the same product. A winner is a winner." It's important that people have learned to trust us long-term. That's more valuable than a $1 million a year in advertising." Catherine is a same.

Example 3: <u>Carl</u>, "I guess the biggest difference is the technology and the numbers, too. Overall, it is the same business, same customers. The paperwork is different, computerized. But we're still trying to accomplish the same things day to day, keep the overhead monster at bay." Carl is difference same.

Example 4: <u>Louise</u>, "It seems to me that it changes pretty dramatically from year to year. There's so much turnover in employees and suppliers and new accounts, but it can't be all that different because, I mean, we're still selling the same products or the same kind anyway, to the same kinds of businesses." Louise is also difference same.

This is a review:
Later that afternoon, Jacob and Miller came back together for a brief discussion. Can you ferret out Mr. Miller's process scope and his process relationship? <u>Jacob</u>, "We had a fully day and I've gathered enough information to identify the scope of my proposal." <u>Miller</u>, before you get into detail, tell me what you think of the manager." <u>Jacob</u>, "I'll be happy to do that. But could you tell me about one of your favorite working experiences?" <u>Miller</u>, "Oh that would be hard to do. I love this job." Jacobs, "Then you must have lots of stories. Tell me one

of them." Miller, "Well, I guess the best time I remember was when we got the Dunston contract. It took a hell of a long time, a year, and a few days. And then one of our key subcontractors went belly up. We really had to get our act together to perform. We had guys working up here round the clock for about a week. It was a mess, but we pulled it off."

Jacob, "Sounds like one of those events that really bring a group of people together." Miller, "Yeah. I guess it was our trial by fire. But anyway, what about that manager?" Jacob, "I believe that he has the capability to do the job. He's a bit overwhelmed because of the volume of input and the limited resources he has for dealing with the information explosion. Conceptually, he picks up pretty quickly." Miller, "Okay. That is all I was needing. Can you give me a bottom line on what you think we need? I don't have time now to get into the Nitti- Gritty."

Jacob, "May I ask you a question before I get started? It will help me understand more about your present system failure." Miller, "Sure." Jacob, "What is the relationship between the distributor sales this year and the distributor sales last year?" Miller, "What is the relationship? Well, it's similar from the standpoint of distributor base, but it's grown substantially in volume. The changes were slow in coming . That's why we've been caught without a way to respond. Now we're in a crisis mode. If we don't get a handle on the situation quickly, we're going to have a loss in profit, and that's something I don't want."

Jacob, "Good. That helps me a lot. I believe that we can get a handle on the situation fast. Based on what I saw today and your present capabilities in the department, I'll be able to put a system together that will be similar in many ways to your present function, and with some additional equipment and software, you'll be on top of accounts within a short period of time. Your problems are not gigantic now, and would suggest that timing is very important. I'll put together a proposal tomorrow and deliver it by 4:00. I will also include references and letters from past customers. Is there anything else you'll need before making a decision?"

Miller, "That will work for me. If things check out, I don't think I'll be talking to anyone else." Jacob, "I'll talk with you tomorrow afternoon. Should I bring some apple pastry?"

Answers to the review. Process scope. Mr. Miller is a mixed pattern, more general than specific. He uses very little detail and few modifiers in his answer.

Process relationship. He is same difference. He seems similar and then difference.

You have now reached the end of the book. Clearly, the secret to success with learning this material is to practice, practice, and practice. There is nothing magical about any of this information. It is just a matter of learning. If you really want to learn these techniques, interviewing people and recording the answers and then listening to their answers until you can clearly identify the patterns will make a quantum difference in your understanding. Good luck.

"Selling The Way Your Customer Buys"

It is import to recognized that each behavior pattern can be a standalone skill for identifying *how your customer will ask for the Order*

Author-Revised Edition
Marvin C. Sadovsky, PhD

Email: ms@leadershipstrategy.ms

www.ingramcontent.com/pod-product-compliance
Lightning Source LLC
Chambersburg PA
CBHW020603220526
45463CB00006B/2424